DEA[...]
A WI[...]
FOR [...]

Can you really look into the future for answers about your love life? You bet you can! For centuries, people have consulted the tarot for its incredibly accurate information and advice. Now, these ancient secrets can be yours—whether you're looking for your true love or just wondering where your current romance is headed. Tarot cards can reveal more about you—and your lover—than you even knew yourself!

TAROT: LOVE IS IN THE CARDS is the definitive guide to reading and understanding these beautiful, mystical, powerful cards. With this book you'll find it's easy to do tarot readings for yourself and others—even someone who's far away. And you may learn that love is just around the corner . . .

———————————————————

NANCY FREDERICK SUSSAN is an astrologer who writes about a variety of metaphysical topics. The editor of *Astro Signs*, read daily by upward of half a million people across North America, Ms. Sussan also teaches astrology and counsels a large private clientele.

The Love Life Guides

Starring Your Love Life
It All Adds Up to Love
The Lover's Dream
Tarot: Love is in the Cards

TAROT: LOVE IS IN THE CARDS

Nancy Frederick Sussan

BANTAM BOOKS
TORONTO · NEW YORK · LONDON · SYDNEY · AUCKLAND

TAROT: LOVE IS IN THE CARDS
A BANTAM BOOK 0 553 40026 6

First publication in Great Britain

PRINTING HISTORY
Bantam Books edition published 1989

Bantam Books are published by Transworld Publishers
Ltd., 61–63 Uxbridge Road, Ealing, London W5 5SA, in
Australia by Transworld Publishers (Australia) Pty. Ltd.,
15–23 Helles Avenue, Moorebank, NSW 2170, and in New
Zealand by Transworld Publishers (N.Z.) Ltd., Cnr. Moselle
and Waipareira Avenues, Henderson, Auckland.

Printed and bound in Great Britain by
Cox & Wyman Ltd., Reading, Berks.

contents

TAROT: LOVE IS IN THE CARDS

CHAPTER I

INTRODUCTION

So, YOU WANT TO KNOW ABOUT YOUR love life. You want to know whether this romance is *the* romance or whether your current partner is just another bozo. Or perhaps you want to know whether there's more romance in your future than you currently share alone with a bag of Hershey's kisses. Maybe you want to know if the person who ignited your love life long ago will someday return. You've come to the right place.

The Tarot is a mighty predictive tool, and its accuracy is legendary. As far back as biblical times, people of all strata of life consulted experienced "Readers" of this mystical book of knowledge. These "Querents" came to find answers that would help them make better sense of their destinies and provide insight into the vast and mighty forces of the universe. The beautiful cards of the Tarot represent a series of symbols that describe the various aspects of life, giving meaning to these external forces and the human reaction to them. Often the viewpoint was that some external forces were at work, pulling each individual hither and yon. These symbols do an amazing job of describing all forces of heaven and earth pictorially so that even without memorizing the definitions of every card, the visually aware can often simply look at the cards and derive a very accurate meaning.

A Tarot reading itself is a combination of the cards' meanings plus their positions within the card spread. Thus one card can have many meanings, and the one most important to you is determined by what the card is and where it falls in your reading.

Each reading is individualized. When you prepare to read the cards, you mix them up a bit and shuffle, and though it seems that you are putting them into a random order as you might for a game of gin rummy, you are actually subconsciously arranging them into a precise order so that they will deliver the appropriate message when deciphered. How do you do this? Your subconscious mind, aided by your higher self, has the power to tap into great reservoirs of information, not just about you but about the universe as a whole. Thus your higher self understands you, your past, your problems and questions, and can see probable future outcomes which are then transmitted to you as information via the cards.

It is important to remember that the cards foretell *probable* future outcomes, for there is no one future carved in stone and predetermined for you or anyone. The future is a series of probabilities based on who you are and what your life is like now. You always have choices and the free will to change the course of your destiny. Thus a card reading can be very accurate for the future it predicts, but you can change that future and then obtain a different reading sometime later. For example, if you see a warning in the cards about problems with your current lover, you may decide to slow down a bit, not to wear your heart on your sleeve or to push for too much intimacy right away. This could give your lover some time to grow closer to you and thus you might avert the predicted disaster. Similarly with money, if the cards predict a period of financial trouble coming up, you can take steps to conserve your resources now, before it's too late, and thereby lessen future problems or avoid them altogether.

That is the essential reason we on earth seek information about our future: so that we can improve it, make the most of the positive, and sidestep the unfortunate. Such information gives us greater control over our own lives and puts our destinies where they belong—solidly in our own capable hands. Information is the essential tool upon which our lives can be built, and the Tarot provides this valuable information in abundance. The more you practice reading your own cards or those of friends, the better prophet you will become.

Each section of the Tarot describes a different area of life. The Major Arcana—also called the Major Mysteries, for these cards represent the mysteries of the universe and forces much greater than humankind—deals with deep and powerful symbols of God, the universe, and man. These themes are reminiscent of the hit movie, *Star Wars*, with their symbols of spiritual power, triumph, conquering, and the forces of light, very like Luke Skywalker's "force." Just as Luke became a master in his universe through the tutelage of those wiser than he and through a positive alliance with the force, so does the Major Arcana (the first twenty-two cards of the Tarot deck) offer all of us that option.

The rest of the cards are divided into suits, just as modern playing cards are, and each suit has a different area of life as its concern. Wands represent nature and personal growth; Pentacles describe money and society; Swords are concerned with intellectual activity, battles, and personal power; and Cups govern emotions and love. Just looking at each suit, card by card, offers a story in linear logic of development and growth or the lack of it.

In this book, we have updated the ancient symbols, offering clear definitions of every card in modern language that you can relate to most easily. If you have consulted the Tarot before, asking question about life and love, you may have received answers concerning battles, crops, or journeys over land or sea, hardly pertinent to your modern concerns. In this book, we have translated the messages into a syntax that makes sense to you today, while retaining the true meaning of each and every card—but as it applies to the modern-day reader.

This book is structured to offer information about each card and its basic truths. Then the card's divinatory meaning is explained. In the old days, this meaning reflected the fact that each individual was doing a dance with fate and needed insight into what the fates—or divine forces—had in store for him or her. Similarly, our divinatory meanings help you find the answer to your question, and thus they are addressed to you. That way, it is as though you have an experienced reader by your side, speaking to you personally about each card's meaning as it relates to you.

These messages are designed to help you make sense of your life. We take the positive point of view that you are in charge of your own life and thus play a major part in creating anything that you experience. This means that you have the power to change what you don't like and to fix what doesn't work, through your own determination and with the wisdom of the cards. You may want to take your time with the messages in order to let them penetrate and thus give you the maximum benefit.

It's important to know that each card has one meaning if it appears right side up in a reading, and another message if it is reversed (or presented upside down). And often the message of a reversed card is almost the opposite of the first meaning. You will notice that to the side of each definition is either the symbol **+** or **−**. This indicates whether the card's meaning is a positive one (good news) or a negative one (bad news), giving you a kind of shorthand to help you in learning the meanings during your own initial readings. Those messages with both a plus and minus symbol can be both positive and negative, depending on you.

Your Tarot card readings can serve one essential

purpose: that of making you a better person through the increased self-awareness you glean through the honest analysis of yourself that the cards will inspire. Each card offers a mighty message about the whole of your life, and you can see this clearly by focusing on an important general question—such as, "Where am I going with my life?"—and then drawing a card and reading its message within the context of the question. The Tarot can also tell you many worthwhile things about the other areas of your life. You can learn about job potentials, future trips, residence changes, financial issues, and those involving your personal growth. The deepest information is available through the readings that you learn to do in the final section of the book.

You bought this book to learn more about your love life, and the Tarot is great for that. As you begin to read your cards on a regular basis, you'll see new lovers whom you haven't yet met but who will eventually come into your life. You will see the nature of your romance, be it good or bad, and you can learn about its psychological and spiritual effect on you long before you would discover those effects in real life. Thus Tarot readings can accelerate your personal growth, as they offer you many insights into romance at a speedier pace. If your love life has been unhappy, you can learn why and what you can do to improve it. Even if you don't see the love life correlation upon first reading the message section, you will discover the power of the Tarot to give you the answers you seek through actual readings.

LOVE IS IN THE CARDS

Your first step is to purchase a deck of cards. Many bookstores carry a multitude of Tarot decks. They are all beautiful cards and simply looking at the amazing pictures can be a pleasurable experience. We recommend the Rider-Waite deck, because that is the one most often selected by expert card readers. This deck features a picture on every card, unlike some decks that use pictures only on the Major Arcana and numbers on the rest. With an illustration, it will be far easier for you to associate a card with its meaning.

Once you get your deck, you will want to shuffle it. (Be sure to mix the cards around in a grand heap before actually shuffling, so that they can fall into their proper order—some right side up, some upside down—and all containing your own energy.) Then begin by doing readings for yourself. Soon you will graduate to the point where you can read for friends and lovers alike. At first you'll have to go slowly, stopping to read each definition as you go through the spread. But you will be amazed at how quickly your skill as a card reader will grow and at the wise counsel you will begin to offer yourself and your friends.

This is your chance to become a gypsy fortune-teller. We all know how magical, alluring, and sexy are those with the power of the future in their hands. New people will demand your services all the time, and lovers will delight in the special treat you offer of giving them a glimpse of the future through your special powers today.

Good luck!

the
mAJOR ARCANA

THE MAJOR ARCANA CONTAINS TWENTY-two cards that describe a spiritual journey from creation in spirit to fulfillment on earth. These concepts naturally are huge, for they are not concerned with ordinary life as we know it, but with God, heaven, divine forces, success, peril, deep love, and human mastery. They are larger-than-life symbols of great power and depth. It may be hard for most of us to relate to the visions of perfect joy through Godly perfection, or of total Hell through the lack of it, but it is important to acknowledge their power. These important cards describe all the forces of the universe, and this is the milieu in which mankind must be immersed if we are to survive and triumph.

Remember, these symbols stand for the process of all creation, of which each of us is but a small part. If you find yourself constantly drawing them, perhaps you have a larger-than-life part to play as

8

your destiny. The cards of the Major Arcana are the cards of the great, of the master, of success on a global level, and they may describe you or the forces that surround you, depending on your outlook and actions.

Allow the symbols to work for you. You don't have to believe in the mysticism they represent, although you will gain greater power if you reach for understanding of these spiritual forces. Just let them stand for the powers that be, the winds that blow us all hither and yon, and our place within the giant scheme of all creation.

Tarot has ties to another ancient science: astrology. The astrological correlations of the Major Arcana are listed next to the appropriate card. If you draw a card of the Major Arcana, it could indicate that someone of the correlating astrological sign is coming into your life.

o the fool

THE FOOL.

The Fool is the holiest figure in the Tarot. He is pure energy: untarnished, lacking all experience, but filled with trust and enthusiasm for the journey on which he is about to embark. Purer even than a newborn babe, he is a soul just created. He has never been incarnated before, thus he has no karma, which is a result of life experiences through the centuries in successive incarnations on earth. The Fool is a symbol of mankind and of life on earth, but at the very beginning, like Adam and Eve, who were new, pure, and totally without experience and knowledge, but receptive to all life had to offer.

Although many are confused by his label, The Fool is not foolish. He is merely without preconceived notions or prejudice of any kind. He is open to receive whatever the cosmos may send him, and that is why he is a holy figure. He is here to teach us all a lesson of trust. The Fool inspires us to trust in God and in the forces of light. With those forces held highest in our hearts, only good can manifest.

+ To draw The Fool in a reading is to reach for guidance. You are seeking the elemental purity with which you began existence and which can help you evolve to greater heights. You know that there is wisdom available beyond your own consciousness, and that is what you seek—inspiration.

− The Fool Reversed is a warning to guard against folly, that you must think for yourself. Spend some time considering your undertaking and then decide wisely.

ɪ the magician

THE MAGICIAN.

The Magician is a card of power and glory. He is a master of the forces of the universe, a pure spirit who, while not of the earth, is here on earth to work his magic and imbue the earth with powers of greater magnitude than the purely physical. The Magician is a link between heaven and earth. He represents the promise to us all that we can master the earth and carve out our own destinies, because we have the freedom and the power to do so. All of creation is a process of spirit enlivening matter. The Magician is a master of this process, for while he understands matter, he is also imbued with the power of spirit. Thus he can take his vision, whatever it may be, and create it here on earth. This is the same process that we all use when we have a dream that means something to us; by focusing constantly on our vision, and by hard work, we make it come true.

The Magician is here to inspire us. We, too, can manifest our dreams in physical reality. To do so, we must replace selfish concerns with a desire to seek the greatest good, to open our hearts and minds to inspiration from God and the forces of light, and to put the information to good use. There are forces on earth that allow us to do anything, and The Magician symbolizes these forces and the mastery within the universe that they bestow.

+ To draw The Magician in a reading is to have great power within or around you. You can be a master of the universe, or you can attract such a powerful individual into your life.

— The Magician Reversed is a warning to release ego concerns and to purify your heart; if you don't, danger may follow.

II the hIGh pRIestess

THE HIGH PRIESTESS

The High Priestess is the guardian of all spiritual forces and has the knowledge of how to manifest them on the earth plane. She is the female, or yin principle of God, for God possesses more than just purely masculine energy. The emotional, receptive, sensitive side of the heavenly forces is symbolized by The High Priestess. She understands potentials and the way things will be, depending upon what energy is put into their creation. She is a symbol of eternal wisdom, understanding, and the purest of love. She inspires us all to hold God in our hearts, and let love be the radiating forces of all existence and subsequent creation and therefore realization of earthly perfection. She inspires us to see the good in all that surrounds us, and to encourage that good to multiply.

The High Priestess is a figure of serenity and knowledge. She is the pure goddess that lives within each and every heart. Although she understands how all things work, she is more an inspirational figure than an active one. Through her knowledge and wisdom, we are all enriched and guided.

+ To draw The High Priestess in a reading is to seek and receive guidance and inspiration. Perhaps you can be the source of inspiration for another— a lover or student who will look up to you and benefit from your wisdom and purity.

– The High Priestess Reversed is a desecration of the values she embodies. Beware of purely physical, sensual pleasures. Dig more deeply and find truth, beauty, and love, not just temporary enjoyment without meaning or value.

III the empress

THE EMPRESS.

The Empress is truly a symbol of the earth, like Mother Nature. A symbol of fertility, love, productivity, and abundance, she is filled with joy and happiness, for she is in her element in the earth plane. She is the happy mother of smiling children, the satisfied artist, rewarded for his creation, the home filled with light and love.

The Empress is a reminder that earth is a place of joy and nourishment, that we all can have in abundance whatever we need, desire, or deserve.

13

She reminds us of the flow of life that we all experience as we travel the journey of our individual lives. Within each life there are seasons that bring us from periods of growth to periods of realization. The harvest that symbolizes the bounty of the earth and our realization of rewards while on it is the province of The Empress. She presides over all and fills the blooming of life with the spirit of love that makes it all so meaningful.

+ To draw The Empress in a reading is to receive joy and love. You may be ready to create a home, to start a family, or to add a new child to an already existing family. Your endeavors will be filled with joy and your life rewarded by abundance. If you are creative, you may be about to receive material wealth as your reward for sharing your art with the world.

– The Empress Reversed bodes trouble. Be certain that your material circumstances are not in jeopardy. Don't waste what you already have but rather conserve. Have respect for the bounty of the earth and for your blessings.

IV THE EMPEROR

THE EMPEROR.

The Emperor is, quite logically, the mate of The Empress, and he represents the masculine, or yang, energies of joy and abundance on the earth plane. He stands for material success, knowledge put to good use, mastery over the physical realm, and the continuation of the species. Like The Empress, The Emperor makes a life here on earth. He works to succeed, and molds the future through his dreams. He makes the world a place in which we are all safe and happy to live.

Through The Emperor, we learn that it is possible for mankind to dominate the earth, and to make the planet's resources pay off for us all. There is a place for each of us here, and it is The Emperor and his principles that make this order possible.

+ To draw The Emperor in a reading is to reaffirm your own power, or to acknowledge that the mate you have or seek will represent this positive force for achievement, power, mastery, and paternity. You are seeking a positive role within the universe, and you will take your rightful place within society and your own home. You will create a world that supports your personal and professional efforts.

− The Emperor Reversed is a sign of diminished power. For whatever reason, you or the man in your life have not yet taken on the true mantle of power. Others are interfering in your life. Seek wisdom and guidance before acting.

v the hierophant

TAURUS

THE HIEROPHANT

The Hierophant is a ruler, like a beloved and benevolent elected official who, through his very ties to the mainstream, is at once a leader and a compatriot. He represents the forces of religion, society, and tradition that define the lives we lead on earth. He is a symbol of earthly ritual, the sense that it is through ritual and ceremony that we here on earth can partake of the power of spirit.

Many can follow The Hierophant, for unlike The Magician and The High Priestess, who represent more spiritual realms, his teachings are relevant to and comprehensible by the masses. He is a figure within society, not above it. Their teachings require a master; his are available to everyone. The Hierophant helps us to create an orderly society with rules, logic, religion, and all the tenets that allow group living to work and to work well.

+ To draw The Hierophant in a reading is to align yourself with the group. Perhaps you are seeking approval or sustenance from others. Your ties to society are strong, and you can find support through the group to which you belong. You like to conform and will be rewarded for it.

+ The Hierophant Reversed can still be positive if you use the energy wisely. You are seeking a newer, more unconventional philosophy than those which have been around for so long already that their worth seems diminished. You want to carve a new path, to find new solutions, and thereby create a new order that ultimately will replace the old. Do this with thought and care. Forget superstition; you know your path. Follow it.

VI the LoVeRS

GEMINI

THE LOVERS.

The Lovers is a card of mystical completion, calling for true understanding of the self, on all its levels. Through that self-knowledge comes the ability to choose total interaction, on a mental, emotional, and physical level. It is the card of fruition on the earth plane, for it signifies the deepest, most total happiness for those who inhabit the earth.

The Lovers calls first of all for development of the self, asking us to acknowledge and develop all the parts of our own unique beings. Then we are offered the soul mate who will provide the perfect

17

complement to us here on earth. We are counseled not to lose our individuality, nor to merge so completely with this mate that we do so, but rather, to join together in a union of strong, complementary individuals that is enhanced by each other's presence.

With this union of soul and mind comes also the union of bodies, for The Lovers promises total fulfillment on all levels—when the conditions are met. Awareness, honesty, independence, and openness to love bring a true soul mate.

+ To draw The Lovers in a reading is to predict a potential love affair. It is up to you to make sure that your romance has the positive qualities described earlier and isn't just an affair of the flesh. Seek a soul mate.

− The Lovers Reversed is a warning to examine your relationship. Have you made a suitable choice and fulfilled the preceding conditions? Avoid temptations and the desire to have a cheap affair. Choose only what is really meaningful and will enrich you on all levels.

VII the Chariot

CANCER

THE CHARIOT.

The Chariot is a card of true power, but power of the earth, not of the spirit. There it differs from previous cards describing masculine domination. The Chariot implies success here on earth by sheer determination, physical force, or mental ability. It is the card of one who succeeds within his element, with the blessings of the divine, but not because of divine power, but rather his own. The Chariot is the card of the warrior, and though he succeeds and often wins, he may not have the divine inspiration or knowledge of the more powerful cards. Instead, he has earthly abilities. It is nevertheless a card of greatness, courage, personal strength, and the determination needed to bend the forces of the earth to one's own will.

+ To draw The Chariot in a reading is to indicate success in your undertakings. You have the ability to make good with whatever you attempt, particularly if you exercise self-control and ask for guidance from the forces of light. A lover may be coming who will embody such forces. You will be surrounded by powerful people who can look to you as a leader or who can help you with your goals.

— The Chariot Reversed is a sign of weakness, and may indicate a need to return to healthier values. Winning at any cost is not a true victory; even if gains result initially, losses will follow. Develop ethics and follow your true beliefs to a righteous course. Then you'll be rewarded.

VIII Strength

LEO

STRENGTH.

With the knowledge that we are surrounded by love, we can take any risk and sail along safely, protected by the divine. Strength reminds us that God is always with us. Since God dwells inside each and every one of us, we can reach inside for that divine protection, even to the point of putting our head inside the mouth of a lion and knowing that we will survive. Reach for your own divinity and let this powerful positive force guide you, for then you can tame all negative inclinations—both internal and external. You will not only survive, but succeed on the highest level, finding true joy, happiness, and complete comfort in your place in life and with your own body and soul. There is more to life on earth than the merely physical, and by reaching for the spiritual part of yourself, you can have even more physical rewards than you might otherwise experience.

+ To draw Strength in a reading is to reach for or acknowledge your own spiritual growth. You have within you the power to direct your own life in the way that matters most to you. Stick with what you know in your heart to be true, and you will succeed. Release all negative feelings, encourage only what is positive inside yourself, and your life will be as you wish it to be.

− Strength Reversed calls for a new influx of positive energy. Work to develop your own character. Don't seek the easy way out or meaningless solutions. Release your fears and trust that in your heart you know the right approach. Ask for guidance if you need inspiration.

IX the hermit

VIRGO

THE HERMIT.

The Hermit is both a student and a teacher. He is a humble figure who stands ready to receive the wisest counsel from above and in turn to share his deepest wisdom with anyone who needs it. The Hermit inspires us all to reach for greater insight and always to be available to help those who have not yet reached our own level. He is a symbol of pure humility, for although he is a true intellectual master, he is aware that there is an infinite amount of truth still beyond his grasp,

21

and he awaits the inspiration that will offer him greater depths of learning without ego or personal demands. Similarly, he gives without thought of repayment. To serve is enough, for all living things, whether in spirit or on earth, come closest to God through the act of pure service and unselfish giving of whatever is needed by those less fortunate.

+ To draw The Hermit in a reading is to seek—or perhaps to offer—greater wisdom. You may receive spiritual counsel or practical information. Whatever comes will help you continue your journey with an enhanced skill to succeed and to help others do the same. Be discreet if you receive a secret—earn the trust placed in you by others. Open your heart to receive what you need, and trust it will come.

− The Hermit Reversed is a caution to pay better attention. Grow up! It's time for you to mature and to take on greater responsibilities. Turn your attention to the needs of others, and you will be rewarded if your heart is pure and you give willingly.

x the wheel of fortune

WHEEL of FORTUNE.

The Wheel of Fortune is a card of universal power. It represents the winds of fate, the course of destiny, the flow of the universe in its ever-changing melee of patterns that are combined, broken down, and recombined in new pictures eternally. These are the forces that affect our lives, and for those not in charge of their own destinies, those forces will blow their lives about without their permission. The Wheel of Fortune is a seductive force that often draws the weak to it, because they refuse to invest energy in their own power and in the divine light that lives within us all. When we work in conjunction with the Wheel of Fortune, everything we desire can be ours, but when we abdicate responsibility to it, we are in for an exciting, devil-may-care ride. With the proper spirit of divinity, we may grab on to the The Wheel and allow it to propel us in the right direction—as long as we know what that direction is and remain always centered and focused.

+ To draw The Wheel of Fortune in a reading is to predict good luck. There may be changes, but usually they will be for the better. Seek and receive an abundance of all things, but beware of excess in

23

your love life, for although it can be exciting, it is not productive or enriching.

— The Wheel of Fortune Reversed indicates failure or at least problems. Examine your life, because changes may be necessary. Are you truly in charge of your own life? If not, beware, for you are in for some trouble. If you are not getting what you want, change your course of action and things will improve. Don't drift.

XI JUSTICE

LIBRA

Justice is a card of balance. It symbolizes our divine right to make the correct choices and thus to formulate a well-thought-out life plan that will produce happiness, harmony, and peace. Justice is the inspiration for mankind to behave in a Godlike manner and then to enjoy the results of goodness, clear thinking, and a heart in the right place. This card reflects the natural order of the universe in which all things are balanced, each in its proper place within the larger scheme of things. It implies that we, too, can absorb and manifest that orderliness; by keeping the spirit of justice at our center, we have the power to create our own world in as orderly a way as the universe functioning around us. Justice implies that the right choices will be made—that it is more natural to make them than to avoid them.

+ To draw Justice in a reading is to seek balance and order. If you are awaiting an outcome or judgment, the decision will go in your favor. You are on the right side. Adhere to the principles of honesty and love, and try to lead a balanced life, and you will be rewarded, for the forces of the universe will be on your side. A career in law could be indicated, as could a successful romance that produces harmony and peace within you.

− Justice Reversed indicates that you are on the wrong track. You may experience defeat, but don't despair. Take it as a warning to change your course and then things will improve. Be sure to be honest and fair in all your dealings. Avoid romantic entanglements based on impure motives.

XII the hanged man

The Hanged Man is at once part of the earth plane and an instrument of the divine. He is not completely in charge of his own life, but that's okay, for he recognizes that by yielding himself up to the guidance and inspiration of higher forces, his own decisions will be made easier. He is a rather meditative figure, relaxing and seeking what he needs in a moment of quiet. It is important to note that although he is not terribly active, he is readying himself to take action. But first, he requires rest in which to recognize the inspiration and influence of the divine. Then he will be better equipped to continue his journey. The Hanged Man has a measure of wisdom already, but his greatest asset is the knowledge that he is not a force unto himself but one who draws power from the infinite.

+ To draw The Hanged Man in a reading is to suggest you need a rest. Take some time off for relaxation and meditation. Seek guidance and wisdom beyond your own. You may be about to move into a new phase of ability, knowledge, or perception. You may have psychic powers. Trust in the spirit that guides you.

– The Hanged Man Reversed warns of preoccupation with earthly matters that are not wholly positive. Release your ego and the sense that you know it all. You don't, and this attitude may be the root of your problem. Seek guidance from your higher self before proceeding with the current project. You don't want to waste your time, so be sure that you are moving in the right direction.

XIII death

SCORPIO

Most people are frightened of Death, because they take its meaning literally and feel that their lives are in danger. Although Death can occasionally predict physical death, it is really a card of change and transformation. In fact, there is no real death in the universe, for as one thing ends, another begins. This is the meaning of the card. Transformation is at the heart of everything in the universe; without it there would be no progress. Death is a card of transformation. It describes the process of releasing the old, whatever that may be: physical reality, mental attitudes, personal relationships, or any current condition. Once this release is accomplished, new beginnings come about. Although letting go is often painful, it is really through resistance to letting go that the pain is formed, not the actual release, which is a profound change and a relief. Death is the precursor of birth, and the new is always better than the old, or it wouldn't be replacing it.

+ To draw Death in a reading is to predict a drastic change. You have been clinging to something that no longer serves you. Soon it will be gone. If you release it willingly, consciously, and with the desire to aid this process, it will be a speedier, far more pleasant transformation. You are at a turning point. Congratulate yourself on the progress you've made so far, then move on.

— Death Reversed is far more serious. Perhaps you are blocking change and therefore feel a sense of greater upheaval than you think you can bear. Don't do this, because you are only making things worse. Be patient and let change happen.

XIV Temperance

TEMPERANCE.

Temperance is a card of balance, peace, joy, and happiness attained through mastery and knowledge of the self. The figure depicted on the card is an angel, and he represents the state of grace to which we can all aspire through the positive fulfillment of our earthly journey. Temperance symbolizes moderation— choosing thoughtfully and appropriately in every circumstance—and skill, for the angel is totally at home wherever he is because he's at peace within himself. We must all seek the inner peace this angel reflects. We need to reach a balance between our earthly needs and our spiritual side; our emotions and our intelligence. By harmonizing these diverse parts of our beings, and not letting any one supersede the other unreasonably, we achieve the balance that results from such a wisely moderated life-style. And we, too, can become like an angel, happy, peaceful, and surrounded by a guiding light.

+ To draw Temperance in a reading is a sign that you are on the right path. You are doing a good job and will be rewarded with success in your endeavors. You are the master of yourself and a servant of others, and thus you create your most important visions harmoniously surrounded by those who will aid you. Expect fulfillment.

- Temperance Reversed indicates that things are somehow out of whack. There is disharmony surrounding you, and you will have to restore your affairs to their proper order before you can make progress. Don't let selfish concerns mar your life. Release negativity and return to a path that feels peaceful and appropriate.

xv the Devil

CAPRICORN

THE DEVIL .

The Devil is a card of earthly problems. It indicates a lack of the balance of harmonious forces described in the previous card, Temperance. The Devil requires us to learn our lessons, for only then can we move beyond his limited scope. He stands for the rules of the earth, which must be followed, brick by brick, if we are to succeed. Often he indicates delays, problems, or obstacles. But that is not a sign that we are being punished by divine forces, but rather that we have not reached high enough to allow them to partake of our lives. The Devil is for those who refuse to believe in the forces of light, which can aid us in our triumphs and make even despair meaningful and bearable. With the Devil, everything must be done thoroughly, and there is a strong call for responsibility and care.

— To draw The Devil in a reading is to predict problems, delays, or obstacles. You have not been thorough enough, and now you will have to concentrate on making improvements. You may have married for the wrong reasons, and now you will have to work out your differences with your mate. Or, you may not get what you want. But remember, you always get what you truly need. Release your ego and let the forces of light guide you to

30

better choices. You can be free of your burdens once your lessons are learned.

+ The Devil Reversed is a positive sign. You have made progress. The narrow concerns that once absorbed you are being replaced by broader, more positive points of view. You can have more love in your life and your heart.

XVI the TOWER

THE TOWER.

The Tower is a card of pure disaster, containing much of the significance that people wrongly attribute to Death. The Tower is like the Tower of Babel in the Bible—a structure built for the wrong reasons and therefore doomed to destruction. This card signifies anything done out of impure motives and the disastrous result to which such actions will necessarily come. Nothing false, completely material and lacking in spirit, or motivated by evil ends can last for very long. Inevitably, disaster will come to remove such an obstacle to peace and love from the earth. There is one saving grace, however—the insight provided as a result of having to experience destruction. That insight gives us all the chance to begin again, to move in a more beneficial direction and therefore to succeed and triumph.

31

— To draw The Tower in a reading is to predict disaster. Whatever you have been doing is an extremely bad idea and you should reconsider immediately. Don't be overly concerned with your own ego, and don't act in purely selfish ways, for you will not be rewarded for this, no matter how clever you are. Release your current course now, and look for the insight that will guide you in a better direction.

— The Tower Reversed is slightly better, but it still is not good. Once you have released whatever negative mind-set was causing the disruption in your life, things will improve, but you will still have to make sacrifices, and it won't be easy.

XVII the STAR

AQUARIUS

THE STAR.

The Star is a card of pure inspiration. Most of us think that our own creativity and intellectual insights come from somewhere inside ourselves, but that isn't so. All inspiration comes from God, and we here on earth act as divine lightning rods who receive His insights. Then we are free to use this inspiration to create whatever we wish. The Star symbolizes this process of inspiration and resultant creation. All we need will be provided to us, and we can receive vast stores of information beyond even that by simply opening ourselves up to receive cosmic inspiration. With this inspiration comes love, peace, harmony, and the total fulfillment of our own natures within our sphere of existence.

+ To draw The Star in a reading is to receive a message of love and inspiration from the spiritual forces that surround you. Many in the spirit world love and count on you to be their link to earthly reality. Perhaps you can be a mystic, a medium, or a psychic who will pass along these divine messages to the rest of us on earth. Open your heart to love.

− The Star Reversed suggests that you have been a doubting Thomas long enough. Stop blocking the information that is there for you to receive. Open up and you'll feel a lot better. If you'll stop being so stubborn and insular you won't have to be alone anymore. Release negative attitudes because they are not serving you.

XVIII the moon

PISCES

The Moon is very similar to the card preceding it, The Star, in that both are involved with inspiration, but The Moon is more creative and far more illusionary. There are many illusions that make up reality, and in fact, there are those who would agree that all of reality is an illusion, for it is the individual product of all our diverse minds and is completely different to each and every one of us. The Moon stands for all illusory forces, including positive ones like new inspirations and creations of art and science, and negative ones such as alcohol and drugs, whose mind-altering properties are seductive like The Moon but which don't offer the chance to create.

The Moon is a deceptive figure, for it is easy to be seduced into believing things that don't quite work. (Look at all the moonstruck aspiring actors who will never see a stage.) It is up to us on earth to choose the insights that work for us from among those The Moon sends out. We must be able to release ourselves to this force of inspiration without letting it control our minds or rob us of our self-determination and the control of our destiny.

+ − To draw The Moon in a reading is often a mixed message, depending on your own state of evolution and degree of self-control. It can indicate

34

great creative inspiration or the greatest of loves. It may mean that you are psychic and able to divine the spiritual meaning in subtle signs for others. But beware of the dark side of The Moon, because it confuses and can deceive you into believing in half-truths.

+ − The Moon Reversed indicates a tendency to cling to practical points of view that can blind you to the seductive, mind-altering lunar properties. You will succeed, but without the inspiration often born of those illusory properties, it may not be a spectacular achievement.

XIX the sun

ARIES

The Sun is a card of success and mastery. It represents the level of achievement we all can reach when we are in complete harmony with the universe and ourselves. Then we are ready to become masters of our chosen field, and we can go out and create the dreams of our minds, hearts, and soul. This is a card of completion, for it indicates the ability to pass beyond the status of initiate—such as that of The Fool—and take up the mantle of the master. Once we have achieved a state of complete self-awareness and total self-knowledge, we can go on to make an important mark in the world, and thereby create our reality according to our own plan, rather than exist as a mere pawn in life.

+ To draw The Sun in a reading is to predict great success and happiness, for you recognize that you have come to the point in life where you deserve it. Not only are you ready to take up your place in society as an adult, but you will form much of what you experience yourself. A mate may come who is your true partner.

− The Sun Reversed indicates that your plans are not resting on a solid foundation, and that there may be some complications. Things may not work out as you had hoped, but this will give you the opportunity to go back and correct the errors or parts of your plan that were ill conceived. If a love affair ends, it is for the best, an indication that this is not your true soul mate. Trust that change is for the better. Similarly, other life changes could offer the opportunity to improve your position if you are willing to accept this challenge.

xx judgement

SAGITTARIUS

Though most people might get an eerie feeling from the Judgement card, its message is a positive one. Judgement represents the complete fulfillment of man on earth as a result of the total infusion of spirit within his being. It is as if we have all become heavenly creatures at last, and are thus now free to enjoy the rewards that previously were beyond our wildest dreams. With the power of spirit as a unified part of our earthly beings, we can go on to make much more of our lives and our destinies than before. All the mysteries of creation are ours to explore and to know, and once we assume this knowledge, we have the power to bring divinity to the earth.

+ To draw Judgement in a reading is to predict success, fulfillment, and happiness. You are ready to live your life with enhanced knowledge, and you will receive rewards as a result. You have reached beyond the petty concerns of others and can be a role model who stands for justice, right, truth, and love. Your projects will work out to your satisfaction. You will win your struggles, because you are on the right side.

— Judgement Reversed indicates a need for some courage. Stop despairing over the way things are going. Your point of view is erroneous, for things do not work out badly when you're on the right track. You may have to release something to which you are currently attached—fear, unhappiness, a partner who does not contribute to your happiness. Don't worry, though. You will feel a lot better when you are free of these limitations, even if it doesn't feel good now.

XXI the WORLD

The World is a card of purest resolution. It represents the successful completion of all endeavors, because spirit is strongly a part of earth. It stands for utopia, the state of perfection. The World symbolizes happiness, harmony, success, and more important, purity. With the complete involvement of spirit, we, too, can become pure beings who live in a state of grace in which everything realizes its highest potential and rewards are ample and justified. The World does not imply a retreat from the earth, however. It is not a card of heaven, but of a heaven on earth in which everything is in its proper place and all things are in perfect relationship to each other. It is a state of complete balance and harmony, like that of heaven, but it exists on earth, for The World describes the successful manifestation of Godly values and virtues here on earth.

+ To draw The World in a reading is to predict the highest of possible rewards. You have traveled far in your journey and now embody many of the spiritual qualities and earthly virtues described in the cards. You will now receive a reward. You may be allowed to reach beyond your own limits to even greater achievement, because you deserve it. Whatever you reach for is attainable.

− The World Reversed implies that you have a way to go before you can achieve success. You are too tied down to whatever conditions surround you, whether they be living space, a job, or a relationship. These things may not necessarily be bad, but they are not the ultimate heights you can reach. Stop blocking yourself. Release the fears that stand in the way of success and happiness.

the
minor arcana

THE MINOR ARCANA CONSISTS OF FOUR
suits of cards, very much like the playing cards we
use today. Each suit begins with an ace and has
nine additional cards, numbered two through ten,
plus four face cards: Page, Knight, Queen, and
King. They depict activities typical of daily life.
There are struggles, wins and losses, need for rest,
love and heartbreak. Each card has several meanings and different meanings when reversed.

These symbols, although not nearly as powerful,
fascinating, or as all-encompassing as the Major Arcana, are easier to comprehend and to relate to in
terms of typical daily life. Although we no longer
exist in societies where war and defeat are major
concerns, it is easy to translate these concepts into
the more modern concerns of conflict and success.
As to many of the other issues dealt with in the

cards—the concepts of progress, of love and marriage, and of needed rest—they are even more immediately clear, because they merge perfectly with our own life-styles in the modern world.

---- CHAPTER IV ----

the wands

THE WANDS AS A SUIT DE-
pict the realms of action and creativity. They are strongly allied with
the astrological element of fire,
representing the signs Aries, Leo,
and Sagittarius. The wand itself
symbolizes the staff of life and the
blooming of nature, for the wands
are always bearing leaves, therefore implying the ever-present
force of life and the ability of all projects on earth
to come to flower and fruition.

The Wands have a benign and agricultural nature. Most of the cards depict scenes within life that
are natural and often comforting. Even when conflict is the theme, there is a sense of playfulness
associated with it—more like a competitive game
than a battle. Generally speaking, the picture of life

presented within The Wands is one of happiness, harmony, gaiety, and most of all, productivity. There is a sense of joy and the potential to have whatever we desire through the successful application of our labors and the attainment of the right frame of mind.

The face cards of the Wands suit represent blonds or light-haired individuals with fair skin or light eyes. This can be in addition to their astrological correlations or instead of them. For example, the Knight of Wands can indicate a pale young man, a pale fire-sign man, or simply a fire-sign man.

ace of wands

All aces signal beginnings, and with the Ace of Wands the beginning is often a creative one. Something new is in the air, or there will be an opportunity to begin something that will eventually flower and produce marvelous results.

+ To draw The Ace of Wands in a reading is to be at a stage of new beginnings. You may be ready to marry or to meet the person with whom you will eventually share your life. New opportunities surround you—seek them in many areas. Do you want a child? This is a possibility now. A new part of yourself is opening up. Look inside for all the potential uses to which you can put this fresh energy. Search for ways to make the most of all your gifts.

— The Ace of Wands Reversed implies delays. You may have thought that you were on the right track, but your plans have not been formed perfectly. That love affair may not be the one you thought it was, or your new business may not quite be all you expected. Take some time to evaluate your situation and where you are going. You don't have to continue in any course that you realize isn't appropriate. Consider needed revisions, and find the courage to make them before more time passes.

two of wands

The Two of Wands is a card of intellectual mastery and material comfort. It signifies the good ends to which well-thought-out projects will come and the rewards bestowed on those who know what they are doing. When we are comfortable within ourselves, the world we create around us will sustain and comfort us and we will become pillars of the community.

✦ To draw the Two of Wands in a reading is a sign that you know what you are doing and that you have the determination to carry your brave plans through to a successful conclusion. You are on the right track. You have thought through your plans and have chosen wisely. Others admire you and look to you for leadership, which you give unstintingly. You deserve success.

44

– The Two of Wands Reversed is a sign that things are not going as well as planned. Sometimes there are hidden problems in any situation, and we can't always be aware of them until they arise to complicate our lives. Such problems may be plaguing you now. How have you contributed to the situation? What can you do to return your life to the right course? Be flexible and give up your egotistical concerns in this matter. Release your fears and other negative preoccupations. Let your own good sense return to guide you.

three of wands

The Three of Wands is a card of success. Once we have set our plans in motion, they are free to be completed and to return to us the successful fruits of our labors. Knowledge and hard work combine to produce success, comfort, and the peace of mind that gives us the confidence to go on to achieve even greater things, built on those that preceded them. There is comfort and joy in the act of surveying our successful creations—that in itself is a reward.

+ To draw the Three of Wands in a reading is to predict financial success. You have worked hard, and because you have put your thoughts and energies into the right project, it will pay off and reward you. Someone with power and money could be coming into your life to offer assistance with your plans. Appreciate the fruit of the earth and the gifts you have received.

— The Three of Wands Reversed is a warning of trickery. Those around you may not have your best interests at heart. Avoid tricky or questionable schemes. Conserve your resources, because there may be financial problems in the future. Seek a more positive means of self-expression and a higher caliber of associate.

four of wands

The Four of Wands symbolizes the rewards we all seek—success, happiness, peace, true love, a partner through life, and the satisfaction of a job well done. There is great joy available to us on earth, and it comes to those who live a good life. Hard work and an honest heart provide the rewards we all desire.

+ To draw the Four of Wands in a reading is to predict love, success, and happiness. You are lucky, and good things will come to you. If a new lover arrives on the scene, this person will be your true soul mate. Or your current partner may indeed be that special person, and you may make a commitment to marry. You have lived a good life, and you will receive benefits as a result. Your projects will bring success, and you can enjoy these rewards as well as the time to relax without worry, for you are on the right track and the universal energies are supporting your efforts.

+ The Four of Wands Reversed is also a good sign. You will have happiness, success, and love, but it may take a little longer than expected, or it may not be quite as spectacular as you had hoped. If you are appreciative of what you receive, however, your attitude may serve to increase your bounty.

five of wanos

The Five of Wands warns of misplaced aggression. It is important to be aggressive, but we all must use our powers wisely and learn the limits of our strength. Sometimes as we grow, we get the chance to test our strength against that of our peers. This challenge can present a valuable learning experience if we approach it with the right spirit and learn the appropriate lesson as a result.

+ – To draw the Five of Wands in a reading implies that you have not yet developed your own strengths and need more opportunities to test yourself. For example, you may have a fondness for competition that is not warranted, because at its base is an underlying insecurity. While you still need to be aggressive, you must learn to control this trait, and this is a lesson you are currently learning.

+ The Five of Wands Reversed is a positive sign. You have learned how to conduct yourself and need no longer engage in unnecessary displays of power. This new sense of personal worth and security in your own power base will bring you success and the possibility of new opportunities. You are on the way to becoming a master.

SIX OF WANDS

The Six of Wands describes the rewards of good leadership, the triumph of a courageous heart, and the camaraderie of those who strive for a single goal. When we are comfortable and happy with our lives, we have the skills to succeed at our tasks and the ability to inspire others to follow our lead. A positive attitude leads to lucky conclusions.

+ To draw the Six of Wands in a reading is to predict success. You may have been involved recently in a tumultuous battle of some sort, and now you will receive your just reward. You are entitled to feel happy and pleased with yourself, because you have done a good job and both your superiors and your inferiors admire and respect you for it. Your hard work has at last paid off just as you had hoped.

– The Six of Wands Reversed is the card of the bad winner. Don't lord your victories over those you defeat or you will inspire them to redouble their efforts against you. This is not the way to succeed. You need to develop a positive attitude and the true spirit of a winner—one who plays the game with ethics and admiration for the sport, whether it's a real game or the game of life. Analyze your own heart and purify it for the future.

seven of wands

The Seven of Wands is a card of courage at great odds. When we know that we are justified in our beliefs and actions, no one can overtake or defeat us. The knowledge of our own righteous position can serve to spur us on to victory; the forces of light will quicken our pulses and come to our aid. That doesn't mean, however, that there will be no fear, for courage is the triumph over circumstances, as well as the fear those circumstances justifiably inspire.

+ To draw the Seven of Wands in a reading is to predict that you will win out over forces that are trying to defeat you. Your position is justified and therefore you deal from strength rather than weakness. No matter what the obstacles, you are in it for the long haul and you know that you will come out on top.

− The Seven of Wands Reversed is a warning to reevaluate your position. You may think that you are safe, but you will face a challenge that you may be unable to meet at this time. Don't try to fool yourself into thinking that everything is all right and thereby justify turning a blind eye to this important matter. You have more work to do and some lessons to learn. Be willing to spot your mistakes, before they cause you losses or trouble.

eight of wands

The Eight of Wands is a card of multiple opportunity. If we wish to succeed, we must reach out in many directions, plant many seeds, make many efforts. Some of these will hit their mark and others will fail, but the harder we try, the greater the chance for success. Although there are indeed many resources available to us all, it is important to have respect for them and not to waste or use them without thought or appreciation. Patience and thoroughness are essential virtues that will cut down on our labor and increase our chances of success.

+ — To draw the Eight of Wands in a reading offers many possibilities. You may be about to travel or to move in a new direction. Something that once blocked your path may now be gone, opening up new opportunities for you. Others may be reaching out to you with information, offerings, or love. Remember to take your time with whatever is involved, because you wouldn't want to foul up your chances through hasty, ill-conceived action.

— The Eight of Wands Reversed is a negative sign. The energy that surrounds the matter in question is negative, and you will have to deal with the results. That could mean disappointment in a lover, a lack of communication with a mate or some other important person, or delays in the affairs that matter. You are in charge here, and somehow you are contributing negative energy. Examine you own heart. What are you doing to sabotage your own efforts?

50

You can change the course of these events with insight and appropriate action..

nine of wands

The Nine of Wands describes continuing struggle. Even after we have experienced a victory, we must be prepared to move along or even to fight again for things that matter. Life is never simple and rarely easy. The strong—those whose determination gives them the power and the inner vision to hold fast to their own beliefs and goals for the future—will win. Therein lies success and satisfaction.

+ − To draw the Nine of Wands in a reading is to say that so far you have done well and that you will probably succeed; but more effort is needed. Strengthen your position and keep after what you want. Shore up your faith so that you have the emotional reserves necessary to carry you through to success.

− The Nine of Wands Reversed implies that there are major problems with your current circumstances. You will have to reevaluate your position if you expect to succeed. Perhaps you lack the proper spirit or the inner sense of security that will tide you over in a crisis. This is usually at the heart of any defeat. Release your feelings of weakness and draw upon your inner strengths, and you will be able to move along to a more positive manifestation of your thoughts.

51

ten of wands

The Ten of Wands is a card of greed. Some people feel that they never have enough, and they therefore invite trouble into their lives. We do not have to grab for as much as we can posibly hold at once. There is always enough for us all, and there always will be. A greedy attitude will produce burdens that will ultimately weaken our chances for success and survival.

+ − To draw the Ten of Wands in a reading is to offer yourself a warning. You may have the strength to manifest great success and wealth, but you are surely not on the right track, and this will reduce your potential rewards. Back off a bit and ask for inspiration. Once you are willing to learn the appropriate lesson and to change your course of action to a more divinely inspired one, you'll stop suffering and move along.

− The Ten of Wands Reversed is even worse. You have really messed up this time, and you'll have some problems as a result. You haven't expressed your best self, and those around you are reacting with the negative side of their own personality. This is a crisis you will have to endure, but your return to the highest possible spirit and the most positive form of self-expression will minimize the pain.

page of wands

Pages are children of either sex, or they can be considered young girls who are potential mates of the Knights. These cards usually refer to a person—not to a symbol of something else—unlike the other cards, which symbolize qualities, activities, or reactions to these things.

The Page of Wands is a fair child with light hair and eyes. He or she may also be a fire-sign person—an Aries, a Leo, or a Sagittarius.

+ To draw the Page of Wands in a reading is to be involved in some way with children. Depending on the rest of the cards and the nature of the reading as a whole, the Page can also represent the arrival of news.

− The Page of Wands Reversed can imply that someone will be bringing you bad news. It can also signal a delay involving children, perhaps that a child is in your future but not in the present or within the scope of the present defined by the reading.

knight of wands

The Knight of Wands is a young man, usually under forty, who is brave, dynamic, friendly, exciting, enthusiastic about his life, and inspirational to be around. Though he is youthful, he is also talented and skilled at his work.

The Knight of Wands is a fair-haired young man

with light-colored eyes. He may also be an Aries, a Leo, or a Sagittarius.

+ To draw the Knight of Wands in a reading can indicate that a man of these qualities will be coming into your life, as friend, business partner, or lover, depending on who you are and the nature of the reading. This man is exciting and dynamic, and he will fill your life with many ups and downs. Though his heart is in the right place, and he definitely means well, it can be hard to count on him emotionally, because he needs his freedom.

– The Knight of Wands Reversed may mean that your lover is on his way, but in the distant future. There could be some delays that prevent you from meeting this man on schedule. Or you might already be involved with a man of these qualities, and the relationship isn't going well. Perhaps you are jealous of his actions or he resents your interference in his life. Whatever the realities, you are not merging as harmoniously as you might.

queen of wands

The Queen of Wands is a powerful woman who feels comfortable being aggressive. She is active, exciting and able to be in charge of many activities, and she inspires others to follow her lead. She likes speed and danger, but she is always in control and never a victim of these things.

The Queen of Wands is a fair-haired woman with

light eyes. She may be an Aries, a Leo, or a Sagittarius.

+ To draw the Queen of Wands in a reading may be simply to draw your own card if you are a woman who matches the preceding description. Or you may be predicting a romance with a woman like her. It depends on who you are and the nature of the reading. This woman will bring joy and activity into your life. She will be successful in running a business or a home, because she is naturally industrious and loving.

− The Queen of Wands Reversed could indicate a delay—that you may meet such a woman in the future. Or you could be having trouble with your relationship with this woman, often because of power struggles in which one partner tries to dominate the other. If she is your current partner, you may suspect that she is being unfaithful, and you may be right. This woman needs a fair dose of excitement and freedom, and you can't nag her into giving them up.

king of wands

KING of WANDS

The King of Wands is a successful, confident man, usually over forty. He has fashioned his life according to his own wishes and is used to others obeying him. He is not stern, however—on the contrary, he has a fun personality. He's just a bit bossy, and can be quite macho. This can be a turn-on as long as he doesn't rob others of their own integrity or independence. He usually has money, often because he made it himself. He enjoys life in the country and being surrounded by growing things. He can be a devoted husband and father as long as he receives the respect he needs.

The King of Wands is a fair-haired man with light eyes. He may be an Aries, a Leo, or a Sagittarius.

+ To draw the King of Wands in a reading is to predict a potential encounter with a man of this type. He could be a business partner, a friend or acquaintance, or a lover. He is lively and exciting, always honest and loyal, and he can bring a wealth of good things into your life.

− The King of Wands Reversed may indicate a delay. Such a man may be on the way but won't arrive in your life terribly soon. Or you could be involved with a man you thought was like this but who turns out to be too high-handed and bossy for your tastes. Don't give away your power to such a lover, for you will soon regret being under his thumb and he will lose respect for you for allowing it to happen.

the pentacles

ACE ♣ PENTACLES

PENTACLES ARE THE LITTLE stars within circles in each of the cards of this suit, and just as they seem, they represent money. They are the symbol of the earth plane, of abundance, of society and of what makes society work, of wealth and that which we all want to acquire to make life easy and rich.

Pentacles are allied in astrology with the earth signs: Taurus, Virgo, and Capricorn. These are the signs that deal with work and the resources of the earth, and Pentacles have some of that flavor. Often the themes in the suit deal with the various aspects of work, whether through reward for successful application of one's labors or of losses through the lack of it. Pentacles provide insight to the flow of life and our own vision of it, of how we view success and our place within society.

For the most part, the picture of life presented within The Pentacles is one of success and abundance and it deserves the respect due all the forces of abundance on the earth plane.

The Pentacles often refer to people with dark hair and complexion. That means that the face cards can represent brunettes, or brunettes who are also earth-sign people (Taurus, Virgo, or Capricorn), or just earth signs.

ace of pentacles

The Ace of Pentacles, like all aces, symbolizes new beginnings. There is a law of abundance which governs the earth, which means that there will always be enough of all resources, including money, material things, food, or even love. This card represents prosperity and pleasure, and it reminds us that those things are not just the result of good luck, but are a normal state to which we all can and should aspire.

+ To draw the Ace of Pentacles in a reading is to predict success, wealth, and happiness. You are doing well, and you will be rewarded for your efforts. Enjoy your life and the good things that surround you.

− The Ace of Pentacles Reversed is a warning. You are not making all of the progress of which you're capable. Your material circumstances are in question, and it is likely that you are either doing something wrong or that you have a negative attitude about money, which you will have to discover, examine, and replace. Don't be afraid to take control of your life. Be willing to take necessary risks. Don't cling to the status quo, for that will only prevent you from discovering a better and far richer future.

two of pentacles

The Two of Pentacles is a card of prosperity, abundance, and allowing the maximum into our lives. We all must be flexible enough to let our circumstances grow and thereby to be able to turn our attention toward new things while still helping the old to grow and flourish. We have many capacities for growth, and by developing more than one we can reap many more benefits, not the least of which is an enhanced ability to deal with life. In other words, we can all do more, experience more, and have far more rewards—both material and spiritual—in our lives if we diversify and expand our own interests beyond narrow boundaries.

+ To draw the Two of Pentacles in a reading is a good sign. You are growing, and the fact that you are moving along with your life is cause for rejoicing. Enjoy all the new and exciting developments that occur, and know that you will receive material rewards as a result of your expanded abilities and outlook. You will also learn to enjoy this new life-style and have more time for recreation and social-izing as a result.

— The Two of Pentacles Reversed is a sign that you are too rigid. You feel bogged down by your life and never really enjoy any of it. Stop going around telling everyone to get serious! Life's not that difficult, and you'd be having a lot better time of it if you'd just relax and enjoy yourself. Develop flexibility. Know that you can handle more in your life and reach out to do so. It'll feel good.

three of pentacles

The Three of Pentacles symbolizes the satisfaction of mastery. Once we have become masters of whatever task we attempt, we can rejoice. Not only is there pleasure in a job well done, and in knowing that our services will always be in demand, there is triumph in realizing that we have created something that will outlast our own mortality and stay to enrich the world forever. We must pass on and die, but good work is the joy of the soul for it can live eternally. Because of such skill, we can be assured that we will always be needed and have a place in society.

+ To draw the Three of Pentacles in a reading is a good sign. You have developed your talents well and now can be rewarded spiritually and materially for them. Others will assign projects to you which you will enjoy doing and which will make you richer.

— The Three of Pentacles Reversed indicates that you have a way to go. Perhaps you are a hobbyist at something. That's fine, but don't expect others to support you while you learn. Forget money for a while and concentrate on developing your skills. Adhere to your highest standards and never sell out or sell yourself short.

four of pentacles

There is abundance on the earth, and we all have a right to that prosperity—but we must not make it our whole reason for being. Yes, we can amass wealth, but there must be more than mere money. The Four of Pentacles addresses the danger of miserliness, warning us that although the miser can hoard his wealth, he will never feel that he has enough. In fact, through the act of hoarding, he reduces his chances of gaining even more. Money is an energy that must be allowed to flow through our lives, not something we must choke to obtain.

+ — To draw the Four of Pentacles in a reading is to predict material gain. It is up to you to make good use of this money in your life. You may have emotional ties with money that you need to release before you can move on to attain true wealth. Don't let this positive surge prevent you from attracting real wealth—or happiness!

— The Four of Pentacles Reversed predicts problems. Your attitude about prosperity is negative, and thus you are attracting losses and financial problems into your life. Examine your heart and release the blocks that are causing these problems. Respect money and the things it can buy, and allow yourself to experience prosperity positively.

five of pentacles

The Five of Pentacles foretells the poverty of the soul. There is a law of abundance that serves as the basis for earthly life: Everyone may have money, sustenance, shelter, happiness, and love. The only thing that can prevent the acquisition of these things is a belief that they are not possible. The Five of Pentacles describes what happens when we block the positive. There can be an abundance of all things available, but it goes unnoticed. All wealth must start first in the spirit.

— To draw the Five of Pentacles in a reading is to indicate that you have a problem with prosperity. For some reason you refuse to allow yourself to fully enjoy life. Therefore you can be without a job, a home, security, or your true love because you believe such things are not available to you. You're wrong. They're out there, and you will have to re-orient your mind and heart if you are to find them. Do it now.

+ — The Five of Pentacles Reversed indicates that you are making progress. You have released some of the negativity that was causing you problems in the past. Others may now be helping you, and things have definitely improved. But don't stop yet; because you still have quite a way to go. Don't settle for anything less than prosperity, joy, and true love. Keep working until you find them.

six of pentacles

The Six of Pentacles is a card of justice. We all will receive whatever we deserve. Whether on the giving end or receiving end, we must all recognize that we are part of society as a whole and must offer to help in whatever way we can to make it better for all.

+ To draw the Six of Pentacles in a reading is a sign that you are on the right track and that those who surround you are honest and have your best interests at heart. You will receive what you deserve, because you have done well.

— The Six of Pentacles Reversed is an indication of serious problems. Those around you may be planning to take advantage of you, and far from being the innocent victim, you may have done something to incur their hostility. Clean up your act! Act only with the highest motives and always be completely honest. This will enable you to attract similar energy.

seven of pentacles

The Seven of Pentacles represents the need to stop and reflect on the meaning of life and on particular courses of action. We must all take the time to make sense of our lives and to develop both a personal philosophy and a philosophy about life in general. Success is generated by three things: hard work, being on the right track in the first place, and believing that we deserve it. When things don't work out, it's because we are somehow not meeting one of these three conditions.

— To draw the Seven of Pentacles in a reading is an indication that your efforts are not going to be successful. It is up to you to stop and examine your life in order to discover which of the three ingredients you are missing. Most often people are on the wrong track without knowing it. The losses will force you to recognize the ingredients missing in your life and point you in a new direction.

— The Seven of Pentacles Reversed is very similar. Things are just not working out. Maybe you put a lot of effort into them already and want to continue despite your misgivings. Don't do it. You know what they say about beating a dead horse. Cut your losses now and move on.

eight of pentacles

The Eight of Pentacles describes the joy of learning a skill. Whatever we do requires time and effort, and within that process of learning and doing is a great pleasure. Through learning we grow as individuais and are able to enjoy the feeling of personal progress. A time of study brings enjoyment, for then we can focus totally on our interests without worrying about the sale of our labor. The only true reward is the pure one of seeing our personal growth as we take on the mantle of the master through concerted effort. Only time will tell if we actually achieve that level of mastery, but it is a pleasure and a privilege to try.

+ To draw the Eight of Pentacles in a reading is to acknowledge that you are working toward a goal. You are in the middle of an undertaking, and although you don't know yet how it will turn out, you are doing your best to make it a success. If this particular project doesn't turn out to be your life's work, that is okay, too. Just continue to develop your skills until you become a master or until you receive inspiration to go in another direction.

— The Eight of Pentacles Reversed is a warning not to prostitute your skills. Don't sell out just for money, and don't assume that just because you are good at something you should do that for a living if you don't truly enjoy it. Instead, be determined to make a living doing something you love and hold out for that. Don't accept poor imitations. Wait for true joy and true love.

nine of pentacles

The Nine of Pentacles is a card of completion. It is about creating a perfect life on all levels for ourselves. Each individual must do this himself or herself, because no one can give a perfect life to another. Not only is material success the logical end product of marketing our highly developed skills, but it is also the result of developing important inner virtues and the completion of the self that stems from honest growth on all levels. Only after we have become complete human beings, fully able to care for ourselves, are we eligible to find a soul mate and to share life, love, happiness, and material wealth.

+ To draw the Nine of Pentacles in a reading is to predict success. You have done a good job, and now you can enjoy the rewards you deserve. You have success, knowledge, and the capacity to understand yourself, to enjoy your own company as well as the rewards you've earned.

− The Nine of Pentacles Reversed indicates that you are insecure. There are some problems that you will have to solve. What is in jeopardy and why? Examine all aspects of your life and see what needs shoring up. Be cautious and take your time in structuring your life.

ten of pentacles

The Ten of Pentacles follows the Nine quite logically. It describes the good life shared with those we love. Once we are successful individuals, we can find a soul mate who is also successful and then together create a happy home and family, and a wonderful life filled with all the good things that bring joy and happiness.

+ To draw the Ten of Pentacles in a reading is to predict happiness, harmony, love, and a wonderful life within a family structure. You will have money and joy to share with those you love, and you will live together in happiness. There may be a new home or a successful business deal in your future.

− The Ten of Pentacles Reversed is a strong indication of problems. There is disharmony in your family, and you will have to pull together to solve this problem or there will be losses or emotional turmoil. Communicate with others, and offer the love in your heart.

page of pentacles

The Page of Pentacles is a young boy or girl, although some people consider pages young women who are potential mates for the Knights. This particular page is logical, careful, and practical and seems to have quite a bit of earthly wisdom despite his tender years.

The Page of Pentacles can either be a brunette with dark eyes or an earth sign (Taurus, Virgo, or Capricorn), or both.

+ To draw the Page of Pentacles in a reading is to predict that such a person may be in your life or about to enter it. There may also be good financial developments in your future. If you're about to have a child, this child will embody the characteristics described above.

− The Page of Pentacles Reversed may indicate a delay in your meeting with this child. For some reason your contact is beyond the scope of current reading but is still a possibility in the distant future. You may suffer monetary losses, or you may have to spend money because of a child in your life.

knight of pentacles

The Knight of Pentacles is a young man, usually under forty, who is practical, hardworking, logical, and concerned with success. He is stable, reliable, solid, and will probably make money, if he doesn't have it already. He is either a brunette with dark skin and eyes or an earth sign (Taurus, Virgo, or Capricorn), or both.

+ To draw the Knight of Pentacles in a reading is to predict a meeting with such an individual, possibly as a friend, a business partner, a lover, or a potential mate. He may also symbolize money issues in your life that you are currently dealing with.

— The Knight of Pentacles Reversed may represent a man you are going to meet in the future, but who has not yet come into your life. This card can indicate a delay for natural reasons or because you are somehow blocking this energy from your life, possibly because you fear change, intimacy, or sharing your personal resources with another.

queen of pentacles

The Queen of Pentacles is an earth mother, much like the Empress, except that she is more completely human. She is a woman who is natural, who has a way with children and animals, and who makes everyone around her feel comfortable and well cared for. She is careful with money and will make a happy home that sings of domestic joy. She is at ease with herself, her body, and all the forces of nature.

The Queen of Pentacles is a brunette with dark skin and eyes, an earth sign (Taurus, Virgo, or Capricorn), or both.

+ To draw the Queen of Pentacles is to describe yourself or a woman in your life who is loving, generous, warm, and sexy. She may be a lover who is coming to you or a potential soul mate. She may be a friend who will offer help or advice on a professional matter. Or she may symbolize a creative, nourishing aspect of yourself that you have chosen to develop.

— The Queen of Pentacles Reversed may indicate a future intimate partner whose meeting with you is delayed. Perhaps you are unsure about what you want from your life and feel uneasy making long-term plans. She may represent such indecisiveness or hesitation on your part.

king of pentacles

The King of Pentacles is a great success, and he is at ease with wealth and power. Logical, deliberate, and fairly even-tempered, he is involved with business affairs and with making more money. He enjoys the good life and all the pleasures of the earth.

The King of Pentacles is a brunette with dark skin and eyes, an earth sign (Taurus, Virgo, or Capricorn), or both.

+ To draw the King of Pentacles in a reading is to predict that someone of this type will be coming into your life as a friend, a business partner, or a potential lover. You are seeking a serious liaison with a reliable partner who has success and security to offer you.

71

— The King of Pentacles Reversed may indicate a delay in your meeting with this man. You may not yet be ready for the kind of relationship he symbolizes. Perhaps you need more freedom, or resent the possibility of being tied down in any way with one partner.

CHAPTER VI

the SWORDS

THE SWORDS AS A SUIT GOVern the realms of action, aggression, and often, violence. They depict struggles in life and portend danger, death, bondage, or despair. This suit counsels us to take charge of our own destinies and control the forces that surround us, seemingly preventing progress. Swords are allied in astrology with the element air, representing the signs Gemini, Libra, and Aquarius. The air signs have a sense of movement and action in common with this suit, but little else; air signs are social and communicative, and that is quite different from the nature of Swords.

The most dangerous and least happy of all the suits, Swords signify disaster more than anything else. In almost every case the upright meaning of the cards is negative, and occasionally so is the reversed meaning, leaving very few positive messages as a result. Swords call for bravery, action, and determination, and they are useful as predictive cards, for they tell us if we're on the right track in no uncertain terms. A preponderance of Swords in a reading indicates either a need for more aggressiveness or a nature that sees strong or violent action as the only solution to every dilemma.

The face cards of this suit represent people with brown hair and/or brown eyes—darker than the blondes of Wands and the light browns of Cups but fairer than the brunettes of Pentacles. This can be in addition to their astrological correlations or instead of them. A Sword person can be a brown-haired, brown-eyed person, an air sign (Gemini, Libra, or Aquarius), or both.

ace of swords

Like all aces, the Ace of Swords symbolizes beginnings, and that is always a positive sign. Swords always refer to activity, and this is a card of definite action—which can be manifest in a new opportunity to make sense of our lives, to take power in our own hands, or to be of a newly aggressive temperament in a specific matter.

✛ To draw the Ace of Swords in reading is to predict an aggressive new start. You are going to take action at last, and you are determined to go in your own direction. You may be feeling a heady sense of power, and this passion inspires others to respond in similarly intense ways. If you are involved in some kind of contest, expect to win. Many triumphs can be yours now.

– The Ace of Swords Reversed warns against unnecessary aggression. You may win through overpowering your opponent, but you will not triumph as a result, because something else will come about to ruin your plans. Be careful that you are taking appropriate steps and that your are acting with honor. All action is not necessarily positive. It is up to you to discern what is the truth—and the right course—in your own situation.

two of swords

Power is nothing without the intelligence to use it or the knowledge of the correct path. The Two of Swords cautions us to develop all our mental facilities and to use positive decision-making abilities before resorting to aggression. Even the weakest among us can have great power, but it is not just power that gets us through life successfully. Wisdom must be combined with power, and to develop wisdom we must open our eyes and learn about what surrounds us so that we can make the most informed choice possible and not rely solely on misplaced brute strength to get us through.

+ – To draw the Two of Swords in a reading is to acknowledge the need for greater introspection before taking action. Don't be so hasty. What surrounds you is not beyond your grasp. Seek inspiration and use your mind to make sense of your situation. Then take appropriate action.

+ − The Two of Swords Reversed indicates that a period of stagnation may be ending, but it is still not certain whether or not you are heading in the right direction. Any change is not always an improvement. Take steps to put yourself in better charge of your own destiny.

ThREE OF SWORDS

The Three of Swords is probably everybody's least favorite card. Its message is clear and totally disappointing: Things are not going to work out. Whether it is a love affair that is going bust, a lover who has a broken heart in his or her past, or one who will cause us to feel heartbreak, this card signifies disappointment. And though it would seem that its message is confined to love, it isn't, because it can also mean that other things may be doomed to failure—a job interview, a new location, for instance. Whatever the circumstances in question, they're not going to work out.

− To draw the Three of Swords in a reading is to predict disaster. Your romance may end, or you won't get whatever it is you were hoping for. You have but one choice in this matter, and that is to release the thing in question and set your sights on a new course. That way you minimize the disappointments and reach for new blessings.

− The Three of Swords Reversed is still bad but not quite as awful. Things still won't work out, but you have probably had the good sense not to count so strongly on this particular outcome so that your recovery will be speedier.

fouR of swoRös

In every battle, there is a time for rest, inspiration, and renewed energies. We must all take advantage of this time of peaceful inactivity if we are to move forward with new vigor. This is the message of the Four of Swords, and it is easy to see how logically it follows the Three. This is the appropriate course of action, whether after defeat or triumph. We must all renew ourselves for the next challenge, and to do so is a wise and positive step.

+ To draw the Four of Swords in a reading is to indicate that you are about to move on to new and better circumstances. You have released the problems that formerly absorbed your time and energy and are now ready to begin again on a positive track. Allow yourself to receive all the necessary inspiration and reinvigoration from the universe and the forces of light. Things will pick up soon, and you will be ready for these new activities and challenges.

+ The Four of Swords Reversed also bodes well, as long as you are paying close attention to what surrounds you. It is time for action—though you may be rushing a bit too much—and you can now have what you want. Be sure that you know what you are doing and where you are going, for this will increase your chances for greater success.

fIVE Of SWORDS

To win at any cost is as bad as losing. The Five of Swords represents the need to develop ethics and to approach life with a pure heart. Regardless of whether we win or lose, to do so as a result of dishonesty or inappropriate behavior is still to participate in something tawdry, and that should be avoided. Those who lose as a result of another's dishonesty will rise again, and those who win that way can never rest securely, because there will be later, greater challenges.

— To draw the Five of Swords in a reading is a bad sign. You are being influenced by negative energy, and this is causing problems that reverberate in your life. Don't take advantage of others by using unfair means—such schemes will only backfire. Also, do not allow others to use you unfairly—you do not have to sit still and be a victim. Surround yourself with positive energy and white light, and begin to change your life now.

— The Five of Swords Reversed has a similar meaning to that of the upright position, but this time it indicates a greater likelihood that you are the victim rather than the perpetrator of the misery. Cut it out! Take charge of your life, stop seeing yourself as a victim, and develop personal strength. Your life will improve if you do.

SIX OF SWORDS

The Six of Swords depicts the positive outcome from the problems described in the Five. We can release negativity of all sorts from our lives and ask for guidance that will help us move along to a happier life. Others will help when we have developed the right spirit and reach out for their aid. Nobody has to stay in a miserable situation; there is always release and improvement available.

+ To draw the Six of Swords in a reading is to predict improvement. You have had a hard time, but now you are ready to release that negative energy and move on to a more positive future. Remember this event and your own successful handling of it, because it will serve you in the future and help prevent troubled situations from recurring. A literal interpretation is also possible—you may be moving to a new, better home or may be traveling in the future.

— The Six of Swords Reversed requires more effort on your part. You have not yet come to the point where you can cut loose from a troubled situation and move along. You can do so, however, if you keep trying. Release whatever has been at the source of your trouble and clear your mind and heart, readying yourself for progress and positive change.

seven of swords

We can all benefit from the many resources available to us. The Seven of Swords warns us to be sure that we are behaving honorably and not trying to take things that don't belong to us. In other words, stealing something works, but although it may be possible to steal successfully, in the end we will fail and suffer as a result. The easy way out is not necessarily the best, particularly in the long run.

— To draw the Seven of Swords in a reading is to predict potential failure, usually due to unsuitable actions. Develop a greater sense of ethics, or you will be sorry and will have to face additional problems and failure. The highest motives are needed here. Adjust your own accordingly.

+ The Seven of Swords Reversed is a sign of progress. Perhaps you weren't always as positive as you are now, or less ethical, or less honest. Today you are doing better, and you are receiving rewards as a result. Positive energy is essential, since you've adopted a more positive outlook and things are working out better for you. Don't be surprised—this stuff really works!

Eight of Swords

The Eight of Swords describes the resolution indicated in the Seven. It is a kind of instant karma in
which the dishonest are trapped by their own worst
actions, or negativity leads to big trouble. These are
the energies of the universe that will demand re-
compense from those who behave in a negative
manner and try to steal from the cosmos things to
which they are not entitled. It's not a pretty sight.

− To draw the Eight of Swords in a reading is a
call to reevaluate your own life-style and mind-set.
You have been on a seriously wrong track for some
time, and thus the universe is no longer supporting
your efforts. You are surrounded by trouble, aggra-
vations, and the unsuccessful resolution of your
own efforts. On some level you are participating in
this punishment, for you know that it can save
you—it can inspire you to change directions and
take up a better life-style now. Give yourself the
chance to return to positive behavior, and the universe will once again be your ally.

+ The Eight of Swords Reversed is a pat on the
back. You are coming out of the fog at last and can
look forward to an influx of positive energy in your
life. Don't attribute this to blind luck, however. It is
a result of your own new positive thinking and hon-
orable behavior. Keep it up.

nine of swords

We must all feel our emotions, acknowledge our place within the events of our lives, and try to make sense of it all. That is the message of the Nine of Swords. We all sometimes feel despair. We all have certain regrets. There comes a point in life when we must evaluate and understand where we have been. If the journey has been largely negative, this will be a trying time of despair.

— To draw the Nine of Swords in a reading is to indicate that you are in a period of taking stock of your life. The problems that were once buried in your subconscious will now emerge in a conscious state where you must deal with them. This can mean severe emotional turmoil or actual events that cause unhappiness. There is no way out of this problem but to pass through it. Experience it, make changes for a more positive future, and release the old, negative feelings. Eventually you will clear your system of this energy.

+ The Nine of Swords Reversed indicates that you have made progress. You are on your way to a period of healing, for you have released the old problems that once hounded you. Look now toward the more positive future you have worked so hard to create. It will soon be yours.

TEN OF SWORDS

This is the card of the ultimate desolation. It is a sign of complete despair and destruction, always because of the actions of the one in question. There is one good thing about the Ten of Swords, however: It indicates the end—a finality from which there is no recovery. This is a situation that will never work out, and once we have learned our lesson from it, a complete new beginning is indicated.

− To draw the Ten of Swords in a reading is to call for complete regeneration. Not only have you been on the wrong path, but you are now at a dead end. Look around you—nothing's working out. What is your true place in this big mess? It's up to you to analyze the situation and to make sense of it so that you can change your course of action and help yourself up out of this defeat. You can't salvage this situation, but you can begin a new course, if you remove the cause of your difficulties and reorient your thinking or approach to life to a more positive, appropriate one.

+ The Ten of Swords Reversed is a sign that you are on the road to recovery. You have released a lot of the negativity that inspired you to make such a mess of your life in the first place. The forces of light are now with you and will guide you to a better life. Things will work out at last.

PAGE OF SWORDS

The Page of Swords is a child of either sex, or could be considered a young woman who is a potential mate for the Knights. This page is energetic, lively, and often aggressive, whether or not he needs to be.

The Page of Swords has brown hair and brown eyes, or is an air sign (Gemini, Libra, or Aquarius), or both.

+ To draw the Page of Swords in a reading is to predict a potential meeting with such a person. You may be ready to have a child or to have an energetic child come into your life. You may be about to receive a message about changes coming into your life.

− The Page of Swords Reversed can indicate a delay. You may have such a child in the distant future, beyond the scope of this reading, but not now. Someone around you may be acting like a child in ways that negatively affect your life.

the knight of swords

KNIGHT of SWORDS.

The Knight of Swords is a young man, usually under forty, who is brave, romantic, active, intense, and intellectually inspired to take action. He may be a bit hasty and lacking in self-control, but he is exciting and interesting to be around.

The Knight of Swords is either a brown-haired, brown-eyed man, an air sign (Gemini, Libra, or Aquarius), or both.

+ To draw the Knight of Swords in a reading is to predict that someone of this type may be coming into your life, either as a friend, an acquaintance, or a lover, depending on who you are and the nature of the reading. This man is hard to pin down, for although he loves socializing, he is not seeking a steady relationship and may be hard to keep.

− The Knight of Swords Reversed may indicate a delay in meeting such a man. He may be coming into your life in the distant future, or perhaps you are doing something to block his presence in your life. Do you fear commitment and being tied down? Perhaps you will attract him as a means of coming to grips with your own emotional instability. He may also indicate the unsuitable use of power in certain situations. Don't be a bully!

85

Queen of Swords

The Queen of Swords is a woman who is more at home in the realms of the mind than in those of the physical or the heart. She may have problems with relationships or with maintaining a steady relationship. She sometimes appears stern and intellectual, but usually this just means that she is preoccupied with mental issues.

The Queen of Swords is a brown-haired, brown-eyed woman, an air sign (Gemini, Libra, or Aquarius), or both.

+ − To draw the Queen of Swords in a reading may be simply to draw your own card, depending on who you are or the nature of the reading. It could indicate that her negative qualities are part of your problem. Or she could be a woman who will be coming into your life, whether as friend, acquaintance, or lover, depending again on the prevailing circumstances.

− The Queen of Swords Reversed could indicate a delay. There may be some contact with this woman in the future, but not quite yet. You may be blocking her entry into your life for personal reasons. Perhaps she reminds you of your mother or of a woman who somehow withheld herself or her love from you.

KING OF SWORDS

The King of Swords is a strong, unyielding man of great knowledge and power, usually over forty. He holds the destinies of others in his hands and often his wisdom is in demand. He may not have a tremendous amount of money, but he does have powerful allies and wields power over others. He is stable and logical, but he may not be available for romance, either because he has ties elsewhere, or more likely because he simply doesn't want to settle down.

The King of Swords has brown hair and brown eyes, is an air sign (Gemini, Libra, Aquarius), or both.

+ To draw the King of Swords in a reading is to predict a possible encounter with a man of this type. He could be a business associate, a figure who wields power over you, a potential lover, or even yourself, depending on the reading and who you are. Determined, controlled, and authoritative, he can help you with his advice or personal contacts.

− The King of Swords Reversed may indicate a delay in meeting this man, though he may appear on the scene in the future. You may be blocking his entry into your life because the qualities he represents make you nervous or ill at ease. Perhaps you have a problem with the authority figures he represents. Or you may be ready to become an authority figure yourself but fear that you won't be able to act as such with honesty and strength. Be sure that you are ethical.

the cups

FILLED WITH LOVE, JOY, AND total happiness, the Cups are just about everybody's favorite suit. The Cups tell us that bliss is the natural condition of life and that if we are not experiencing this joy, it is because we are not paying enough attention to the opportunities for happiness that always surround us, thereby failing to avail ourselves of this bounty. Cups are allied in astrology with the element water, representing the signs Cancer, Scorpio, and Pisces. Water represents the unconscious mind, emotions, and the intuitive powers we all have at our disposal, and that is just what the Cups are all about.

The Cups embody many instances of pleasure, socializing, rejoicing, love, and celebration. All we need do is reach out a willing hand, and the manna of life will fall into our grasp. The Cups represent a joyous picture of life that is not only the truth, but what we should all seek within our own existence. If we hold the ideals of the Cups in our hearts as the highest potential truth, we will create this beautiful life for ourselves, because we know it is possible, and yes, normal within our own lives.

The Cups usually refer to those with light brown hair and medium or hazel eyes—darker than the Wands, but lighter than both the Swords and the Pentacles. A person represented by the Cups can be as described above, a water sign (Cancer, Scorpio, or Pisces), or both.

ace of cups

The Ace of Cups, like all other aces, signifies beginnings, and this is one of the most pleasurable of starts possible for anyone. This Ace represents true love, divine happiness, and the joy we can all receive when we are held securely in the palm of God's hand. This card can signify a creative beginning as well, whether through a child conceived of great love, a project inspired by the soul, or a masterpiece of art in the making.

+ To draw the Ace of Cups in a reading is to predict the ultimate happiness. The lover for whom you have yearned throughout your life is coming, and you will share the deepest of love and greatest joy possible. Your life is working out beyond your wildest expectations. You are being rewarded because of the good deeds you have done in the past and because you have shared a spirit of love and devotion with those around you.

— The Ace of Cups Reversed is a bad sign for your love life. The partner you think is so wonderful may not be at all what you believe. Or you yourself may be unprepared or unwilling to yield to true love, and so you keep attracting those who do not fulfill your deepest self. Find the courage to allow love to be an important part of your life. Start by helping those less fortunate as a service to society. Open up little by little, and you will be healed.

two of cups

The Two of Cups is not quite a card of true love, but rather of the potential to realize such adoration in the future. It represents the beginning of a relationship, one with a suitable partner with whom we feel a bond that has yet to develop. This card symbolizes the possibility for growth and achievement together, of harmony, peace, and devotion through time, and willingness to come closer together in love. Thus it foretells new beginnings that haven't yet materialized but may be on the way.

+ To draw the Two of Cups in a reading is to predict the beginning of a successful liaison. Although it is likely that this will occur in your love life, it can also mean a meeting with anyone whose energy blends favorably with your own. You are ready and willing to share yourself with another, and this is the proper step for you to take.

— The Two of Cups Reversed means you have a way to go before you are ready for love. You still have some things to learn about your own nature and your own heart. Someone will come into your life to aid you with these lessons, though you may not see it so objectively. Don't cling to someone who would leave you—you can't succeed that way. Strive for growth and self-mastery, not control over others.

three of cups

Pleasure is the nature of life on earth, and we may all experience this joy in abundance. That is the message of the Three of Cups. There are many others with whom we can share happy feelings and personal success. Life can be wonderful, and we need only to reach out for it and enjoy it. Positive spirits contribute to success and create harmony around us.

+ To draw the Three of Cups in a reading is to predict good fortune and fun. You may be going to a party, or you may feel so happy that your life seems like a continual party. You have done well and will experience success, joy, and friendship.

— The Three of Cups Reversed warns that too much of a good thing is not positive. Don't be a slob! Yes, enjoy yourself, but not to excess. That means that two dates with different partners in one day is a bad idea! Similarly, you should avoid high-calorie treats and liquor in excess; you don't want to make yourself sick. It is important to know the difference between abundance and gluttony. This is your challenge now.

four of cups

There is a world of abundance surrounding us, and we must only look to find it. In the Four of Cups, we are asked to pay attention and to recognize how full of joy is the universe that surrounds us all. We must find a responsive chord within our own beings, and that, in turn, will merge with the beauty and wonder around us. Without an inner richness to connect with the outer abundance, we will be left lost and searching. In other words, once we develop all parts of ourselves the world will be an even richer, more wonderful environment for our efforts. It is easy to see how this advice follows from the message in the Three Reversed.

— To draw the Four of Cups in a reading is to indicate that you need some inner joy. You are not in touch with the rainbows inside yourself, and it's no wonder the world looks so gloomy. It isn't your success or your wealth that is slowing you down, but rather a lack of understanding about the true meaning of these blessings within your life. Seek now to understand yourself and your assets. Give thanks for your blessings and open your heart to love.

+ The Four of Cups Reversed indicates that you have done some successful soul-searching. You are now ready to face the world again, more secure in your own heart and thus ready to share yourself with others. You may be about to fall in love or to start a new and more meaningful project.

five of cups

Yes, the world is a beautiful, nourishing place, but it is up to us to receive this sustenance. If we dwell on misery without recognizing the positive things that far exceed all unhappiness, we will not experience the positive. The Five of Cups warns us that misery is born of a miserable inner state. Nothing in the universe can cure a despair-filled heart, if that is what we cling to most strongly. But there can be recovery, as soon as we allow the blessings of the universe once again to be our own.

− To draw the Five of Cups in a reading is to indicate that you are feeling depressed and that you might want to stay that way. You may have suffered a broken heart, and now you feel too desolate to return to the mainstream of life. This is your choice, but remember that wallowing in misery is not the same as receiving a healing balm. Ask for a healing now if you want to be free of this unhappiness. Release old problems. Let yourself be cured and return to life. It's up to you.

+ The Five of Cups Reversed indicates that you are coming out of the shadows. You have decided to put the past in its place, enjoy the present, and create a brighter future. Good for you. Things are working out at last. Your desires are well founded and will be fulfilled.

SIX OF CUPS

The Six of Cups has a strong correlation with the sign Cancer, because it describes the rhapsody of childhood and represents the memories of joy and happiness we can bring into our lives today. Somewhere in everyone's past was joy and grace, a time of peace and being cared for by someone else. These memories give us the strength to become adults and to return the favor, caring for others who need us.

+ To draw the Six of Cups is to indicate that you have a wealth of happiness inside you and that your memories can bring joy and peace to the present times. You may be ready now to start your own family and to make it just as wonderful as your actual childhood was or as you wish it had been.

− The Six of Cups Reversed is a sign that you should move on. If you did have a great past that now is gone for some reason, you can't bring it back by dwelling on it. Work instead to make the present as happy as your past once was.

seven of cups

The Seven of Cups has a meaning very similar to that of The Moon in the Major Arcana. Our minds are wonderful tools of inspiration as long as we don't let them run wild. Without control and a focused approach, we can be witness to all sorts of phantasmagorical visions that don't quite make sense. Similarly, we are free to dream our highest dreams, but we must make sense of them if they are to materialize in our lives on the earth plane. This card is a warning to make sense of our perceptions, visions, and desires.

− To draw the Seven of Cups in a reading is a message to come out of the clouds and start making sense of your life. Just dreaming isn't enough, or things would be working out better now. The problem is that your dreams are blocking you from achieving goals in real life. Get with it! Be practical, and things will improve.

+ The Seven of Cups Reversed indicates that you are beginning to turn a practical eye toward your problems at last. Thus they are starting to work out and make sense. Don't give up your dreams, just their tyranny over you. As long as you are the master of your own mind, success will follow.

eight of cups

As in the Four, the Eight of Cups demands that we make sense of the blessings the universe has bestowed upon us. Material success without the spirit to match, or the love in our hearts to give it meaning, is useless. There may be journeys beyond those that provide material blessings, especially for those whose lives follow a more spiritual path. We assign value to all things in our lives, and for each individual the value may be different. It is our task to seek whatever it is we hold highest in life, regardless of the opinions of others. It is also important to respect and appreciate the things we receive. We should take the time to experience our initial blessings before we seek more.

— To draw the Eight of Cups in a reading is to be in the throes of uneasiness. You have what you once wanted, but somehow it doesn't bring you happiness. Why is this? If it is because you didn't seek your true dream, you are justified in seeking it now. If it is because a shallow attitude prevents you from seeing or appreciating all your true blessings, then you will have to journey in search of the truth that stares you in the face but that you refuse to see. The key is to know your own heart and seek your answers *there* first. You may indeed have another calling, a truer love, or a spiritual purpose that now is made clear to you. Always follow your own path.

+ The Eight of Cups Reversed indicates a new sense of balance. You have found inner peace and now seek the manifestations of happiness, whether they be love, money, or professional success. Choose whatever brings you joy.

nine of cups

We are all capable of attaining our true heart's desire, and that is the message of the Nine of Cups, which promises happiness, success, and the fulfillment of our wants. This is a card not just of luck, but of success in the material realm. It is the card of satisfaction within life and of an existence filled with all that we desire.

+ To draw the Nine of Cups in a reading is to predict success. You will get what you have wanted, and it will make you happy. Your life will be filled with abundance, and you will enjoy the fruits of your labors. Expect love, money, prosperity, and great success.

− The Nine of Cups Reversed is a card of gluttony. Don't be so greedy that it is impossible for you to be satisfied—that will only guarantee your own unhappiness. Don't be so insecure that you have to clutch what you have too closely, because that is a sure way to lose it. Learn to appreciate your proper place in life and to desire things you really want in the appropriate amount.

ten of cups

The joy of love creates a happy family, which will be a thread of positive emotion that is carried through into the future. When we merge our life with that of our true love, this soul mate can become our partner in bliss. Together we can create a joyous existence that is the cornerstone for all the life that follows. We can experience the true abundance of heaven here on earth.

+ To draw the Ten of Cups in a reading is to predict joy and happiness. You have found the right soul mate, or one will be coming soon, and together you will start a happy home and family. This mate will be your perfect complement, and together you will reach new realms of happiness because your union is not just physical, but a merging on all levels—physical, mental, and spiritual.

− The Ten of Cups Reversed is a warning not to throw away your perfect love. Don't compromise and accept shoddy imitations. You will know in your soul when something is right—wait for that moment and that soul mate. If your current partner is not this person, don't force the relationship to continue. To force the situation won't make it work, and it could block your true destiny from unfolding.

page of cups

The Page of Cups is a young girl or boy, although some people consider pages young women who are potential mates for the Knights. This Page is emotional, moody, and imaginative. He or she may be creative, but if not, will surely display a sensitive temperament. This child requires lots of love and attention, and may be a bit secretive at times.

The Page of Cups has light brown hair and light or hazel eyes, is a water sign (Cancer, Scorpio, or Pisces), or both.

+ To draw the Page of Cups in a reading is to predict a potential meeting with such a person. Perhaps you will have a child who fits this description. You may want to work with children, or to get in touch with the child still alive inside of you.

– The Page of Cups Reversed can indicate a delay. You may be meeting such a child in the distant future, beyond the scope of this reading. Or you may be blocking the energy that would signal this child's arrival. If you haven't received enough nurturing of your own, you may not feel ready to be a parent. You may have to become more responsible and adult before you can move ahead in more positive directions.

knight of cups

The Knight of Swords is an artistic fellow, usually under forty, who can be moody, melancholy, creative, and inspired. He has a powerful imagination and can sense the truth in others' hearts without asking for it. He is temperamental and may require an extra bit of your time and attention, for he likes to be mothered.

The Knight of Cups is either a light-brown haired, light- or hazel-eyed man, a water sign (Cancer, Scorpio, or Pisces), or both.

+ To draw the Knight of Cups in a reading is to predict that someone like this may be coming into your life, either as a friend, a creative consort, or a potential lover, depending on who you are and the nature of the reading. Although he may be hard to understand, he can be quite devoted to you, and his affections will never waver, even if time or distance separates you. He likes pleasing you and can be an accomplished lover.

− The Knight of Cups Reversed may indicate a delay in meeting such a man. He may represent your distant future, beyond the scope of this reading, or he may symbolize an affair that binds you but somehow isn't what you want. Maybe you have the hots for a man who doesn't satisfy you. Or perhaps you are afraid of becoming involved with an emotionally receptive partner because you cherish your freedom and fear he will rob you of it.

queen of cups

The Queen of Cups is a receptive, emotionally available woman who is motherly and kind, able to take care of those who surround her. She is a visionary, but she has practical abilities, too, and she can create powerful manifestations of her own mind and heart. She loves art and music.

The Queen of Cups has light brown hair and light or hazel eyes, is a water sign (Cancer, Scorpio, or Pisces), or both.

+ To draw the Queen of Cups in a reading may simply be to draw your own card, depending on who you are or the nature of the reading. If she is you, it may be a sign that you are developing greater emotional stores of receptivity that you share with others. Or she may be coming into your life as friend, mother figure, lover, or confidante, depending again on you.

− The Queen of Cups Reversed could indicate a delay in your meeting with this woman. She may be coming into your life sometime in the distant future. Or it may mean you feel ill at ease with love. Perhaps you are too wrapped up in your own dreams to share yourself with another, or perhaps you fear intimacy. Maybe you were hurt once and now are hesitant. Seek the appropriate answers within yourself.

kING oF cups

The King of Cups is a successful man whose main interest is not money, although he has plenty of that. He has eclectic interests and has worked to develop all parts of himself. He is over forty. Solid, substantial, understanding, and reliable, he is a sensitive friend and a knowledgeable confidant and mentor. He loves children. He helps those around him and is a reliable member of his community.

The King of Cups has light brown hair and hazel or light eyes, is a water sign (Cancer, Scorpio, or Pisces), or both.

+ To draw the King of Cups in a reading is to predict a possible encounter with a man of this type. He could be a business associate, a father figure, a mentor or personal adviser, a neighbor, a lover, or even yourself, depending on who you are and the nature of the reading. He is artistic, generous, loving, and kind and he can share all these attributes with you in a generous and loving way.

– The King of Cups Reversed may indicate a delay in meeting this man. He may be coming into your life in the distant future, beyond the scope of this reading. You may have problems with the qualities he represents. Perhaps you have unresolved conflicts about your father, or maybe you yearn for security and want an older man who will take care of you, allowing you to abdicate your responsibility as an adult. This will not work out ultimately. Be a grown-up now!

CHAPTER VIII

READING
THE CARDS

THE FIRST STEP IN READING THE CARDS IS to buy your own deck and to mix it up thoroughly. The method we prefer is simply to open the deck and to spread the cards in a big heap upon the floor or a large table. Keep mixing them up, swirling them around and together so that some are turned in the opposite direction. Then reassemble the deck and shuffle as you would playing cards. You're ready!

Remember that the reason for a careful shuffle is to inject your own energy into the cards. That is essential. If you are playing gypsy and reading for someone else, he or she will have to shuffle the cards. Simply passing a hand over the deck won't do the trick at all. Let the "Querent," or the person for whom you are reading, reshuffle just as you did initially, by mixing the cards up and around so that some are right side up and some upside down; then have them actually shuffle. This will channel his or her energy onto the deck. Remember after doing a reading for another individual to reshuffle thoroughly yourself so that you restore your own energy to the deck.

The first method of reading the Tarot is called the Keltic Cross, and it is as ancient as it is popular. The first step is to choose a card to represent yourself (or the person for whom you're reading). To do so, read through the definitions for the face cards, and choose the one that seems most appropriate. This is an old custom that was probably started as a magic ritual designed to bring the energy of the person being read into focus. Today, it really isn't essential but can still be interesting and fun. Your "Querent" will be sitting next to you, and thus his or her energy will be present in the room. If you are reading for yourself, the same applies. Even should you desire to read for an absent individual, you can summon his or her true cards simply by clearing your mind of all other thoughts and saying out loud that this reading is for Jack or Jane, or whoever. If you prefer the ritual of choosing a face card, go ahead. Lay it in the center of your reading area. Then shuffle the cards.

In this first example, we are going to do a general reading, though you can ask a specific question if you choose to do so. The cards are laid out according to the diagram below, with each number representing a position, and each position having a specific meaning.

LOVE IS IN THE CARDS

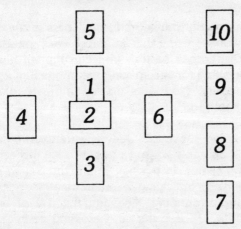

The definitions by position are:

1. This is what surrounds you (or your question), the circumstances of your life.
2. This card is laid across number one, and you should read its right-side-up meaning, not the reversed one. This is a challenge you may have to face.
3. This is the past on which your life is built.
4. This is the present but is no longer a strong influence.
5. This is the potential future.
6. This is coming in the near future.
7. This is your fear or what holds you back.
8. This is the influence of family and friends on your situation.
9. This is your hope and wish.
10. This is the final outcome or resolution.

If you are going to use the Keltic Cross method, you may want to copy this list and have it nearby for handy reference so that you can flip through the book looking for the specific meanings that apply more easily. Now let's do a sample reading using this method.

For Nina, we chose the Queen of Pentacles, because she is an earth sign—Taurus. We lay this card down in the center. In position one is the *Seven of Cups Reversed*, indicating a practical atmosphere of creativity surrounding Nina and the use of her talents. *Temperance* is the card crossing it, in position two, indicating great inspiration and the need to reach even further in her creative growth. Because Nina is a writer, this makes sense. In position three is the *Eight of Swords Reversed*, indicating that Nina has a history of positive thinking and self-determination, which form a strong background for her life and creative self-expression. Position four, signifying recently departed influences, is held by the *Five of Swords*, indicating a recent trauma of the mind or spirit that Nina has suffered. Perhaps she has doubted her own creativity and ability. In the fifth position, representing a potential future, is the *Queen of Wands Reversed*, indicating another delay in creativity and the need for some control. So far it would seem that Nina has what it takes for success, if only she will take control of her destiny and use her resources to the maximum.

In position six, or the near future, is *The Magician Reversed*, indicating a need for Nina to release her ego and to allow the universe to inspire her.

This can also be an indication of innate talent as a card reader, which Nina hopes to develop. In position seven, charting Nina's fears, is *The Lovers*, indicating not just trouble with creativity, but a fear of relationships that may be keeping her married to her work instead of out in the world seeking a new romantic partner. Position eight, representing family opinions, is the *Ace of Swords Reversed*, indicating a tendency for misdirected aggression. Nina's family is filled with leap-before-you-look types, and she wants to avoid this direction. Position nine, representing Nina's hopes, is held by the *Five of Pentacles*, indicating that she is reaching for greater spiritual inspiration from which she hopes to benefit materially. In the last position or final outcome is the *Eight of Wands*, indicating growth and many opportunities coming in her direction. This reading would seem to indicate that Nina is in a period of growth and must reach up to a higher plane of self-expression.

In her second Keltic Cross reading Nina asked for information about her love life. In position one, describing the general atmosphere surrounding her, Nina drew the *Nine of Pentacles*, indicating that she has been an independent, successful woman for some time who now feels ready for a romance. Crossing her is the *High Priestess*, which indicates that Nina may be withdrawing from relationships into the isolation of her work and that others may find her hard to approach as a result of this. In the position of the past is the *King of Wands*, the man with whom Nina recently had a devastating affair and the reason for her current withdrawal. In position four, that which is just ending, is *Death*; this tells us that Nina has worked to release this man from her heart and to ready herself for a new liaison. In position five, or the potential future, is the *Two of Cups*, describing a possible new romance with a suitable partner—Nina is ready for a beginning. Position six, or the near future, is occupied by the *Knight of Cups*, a new man she will meet. Position Seven, describing Nina's fears, is *The Tower Reversed*, or the fear that disaster will follow another affair. Nina is afraid of suffering another broken heart. In position eight, or family opinions, is the *Wheel of Fortune*. Nina's family is supportive and wishes her the best. In position nine, which represents Nina's hopes and wishes, is the *King of Cups*, or the man with whom Nina can trust her heart. In position ten or the final outcome is the *Ten of Cups*, predicting a spectacularly happy romance probably leading to marriage if Nina can overcome her fears and trust in love once again.

Another card-reading method uses astrological houses as position points for the cards. We call this setup the Wheel of Fortune. In the Wheel of Fortune spread, there are thirteen different positions, each with its own meaning. Thus this method can provide a much greater wealth of information than the Keltic Cross. For greater insight, you can combine similar positions for enhanced meanings. The positions are as follows:

LOVE IS IN THE CARDS

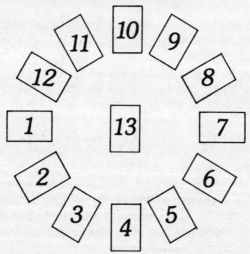

1. You or the person for whom you are reading.
2. Money.
3. Brothers and sisters. Neighbors. Nearby travel. School.
4. Home. Family. Mother.
5. Your love life, romance. Creativity. Children.
6. Work. Health.
7. Your mate. Business partners.
8. Your mate's money. Taxes and insurance. Sex. Passion.
9. Your philosophy. Travel. Higher education.
10. Your career or position in the community. Father.
11. Friends. Groups like clubs. Big business.
12. Secrets. Creativity. Subconscious mind.
13. The outcome. The final meaning.

This reading is for Greg, a ladies' man who has recently been experiencing troubles in both his love life and his career.

In position one, describing Greg, is the *Eight of Cups*. Greg has had a lot of success and love offered to him in the past, but somehow he is not secure or happy because of it. He is still seeking something else. In position two, describing Greg's finances, is the *Queen of Swords*. We would then ask Greg who she might be, particularly because she is in his money slot. She is not his boss, but rather a woman he knows from work whom he dates casually. This woman is a Gemini, and that's how we recognize her, since the Queen of Swords is an air-sign woman.

In position three, which describes neighborhood activities (or more likely here, the general atmosphere surrounding him), is *The Hanged Man*. Greg is in a period of inactivity, through which he is seeking inspiration and information about his life path; this is another indication of the condition described in the first card. In position four, or Greg's home or emotions, we find *The Moon Reversed*. Greg won't let go emotionally, and that is why he has such a hard time falling in love. In position five, romance, is the *Ten of Pentacles Reversed*, indicating family problems or emotional turmoil. Thus, Greg's family history is at the root of his relationship problems—he had severe problems with his mother, even if he refuses to acknowledge them, and that forms the source of his difficulties with women.

In position six, work, is the *Knight of Wands Reversed*, indicating a new job in the future, but not quite yet. In position seven, or his mate, is the *Nine of Wands*, indicating a guarded approach to matrimony. Greg has often said that he feels women are out to trap him into marriage. In position eight, or his partner's money and his sex life, we see the *Eight of Swords*, indicating that his sex life is currently unsatisfactory; and when we tell Greg this he laughs because it is so unusual for him. We point out that it is his own fear of closeness that is at the bottom of this problem, as indicated by the readings in positions one, four, five, seven, and eight. The problems with sex are an immediate flag, trying to warn Greg that he has a bigger problem dealing with intimacy and relationships.

In position nine, or Greg's philosophy and travel, is the *Page of Pentacles*. This is simply a nephew Greg is planning to visit on vacation. In position ten, Greg's career, is the *Two of Swords*. Greg is not sure where he is going in his job, and he is seeking a new position. We point out that he has two choices but must first know where he is headed with his life in general. That is the bigger dilemma, as indicated by this card plus the first, third, and fourth. In position eleven, describing friends or large organizations, is the *Ace of Cups*, a very positive sign. Greg will have a chance to join a large firm in the near future, and that may come to him through the positive influence of a friend. He can expect a measure of emotional support as a result of this contact. In position twelve, indicating secrets or the unconscious, is the *King of Wands Reversed*. We take this to mean the same thing as position six—a new job in the future. There may also be a business partner described by the Wands men, and that, too, is positive. The final card or the outcome is the *Ace of Wands*, a highly positive indication that good things will come about for Greg—including a chance for the personal and emotional growth which will allow him the happiness that has been eluding him. An Ace at the end of a reading is always a good sign: No matter what troubles are revealed by the reading, this final outcome indicates that the individual in question can turn the troubles around to a positive conclusion.

As you can see from Greg's reading, it is not only possible to predict the future with the Tarot cards, but it also possible to achieve deep psychological awareness of both present and past emotional issues. This knowledge is the most essential tool in the creation of a better future.

After doing a reading by the Wheel of Fortune method, it is possible to ask specific questions. Simply reshuffle the first thirteen cards, and then spread these cards out facedown on the table. Speak the question aloud and choose seven cards to answer it. For example, Greg might ask, "What can I do to overcome my relationship problems?" Then he chooses seven cards that we turn face side up. They are as follows:

1. Eight of Pentacles Reversed: don't sell out.
2. Five of Pentacles: Stop refusing to see life as wonderful.
3. Three of Pentacles Reversed: money can't buy love.

4. Three of Cups Reversed: don't be such a glutton—stop having a love fest with so many women.
5. Knight of Cups: this is Greg's card; get in touch with your own emotions and stop denying them.
6. Nine of Swords: take stock, deal with your emotions, and release the negativity from the past.
7. Ace of Wands: begin anew.

While this is a very dramatic answer to a question, it does represent an actual reading. Greg has an attitude problem about love: He doesn't believe in it, nor does he feel he deserves it. It's sad. Greg must release these negative mind-sets and abandon his "love 'em and leave 'em" behavior pattern. He should deal with his past and release it. Only then will his love life improve.

As you can see, the Tarot provides very potent answers that are right on target. You don't have to ask questions as serious as Greg's, however. One card reader always inquires about the weekend. You could ask about your love life, your sex life, your finances, or a proposed vacation. There is virtually no question for which you can't find an answer in the Tarot. It is even possible to ask yes-or-no questions. Simply voice the question, choose three cards, and turn them faceup. If two out of three are right side up, the answer is yes. If two are reversed, it's no.

The one thing that it is difficult to do is to determine

the time frame indicated by the reading. Generally a reading is good for up to six months into the future. Of course, if you read your cards frequently, that may vary. You can't ask a when question, however, because there is no way for the cards to communicate that information. Your ability to read your own future and that of your friends is limited only by your own skill in applying the general meanings of the cards to the specific situation at hand. With patience and practice you will develop greater skills. Enjoy the challenge!

The Tarot contains all the mysteries of the universe, and your life is but one of those mysteries. You are as magical and unique as any of the symbols we have tried to illuminate for you in these pages. Enjoy the process of developing a working knowledge of these symbols. Just thinking about them can be inspiring. If you want to be a part-time philosopher who has the key to the universe and all its grandeur, learning to read and understand the cards is an excellent place to start. Beyond the intellectual stimulation you will receive by contemplating these mysteries, there are other benefits. You will start feeling more powerful, because you will see that you are the center of your own universe and able to create your own, satisfying reality. You will sense that a fulfilling career with prosperous paychecks can be yours if you reach for them. Similarly, you can experience people differently and can receive the light that they can share. Best of all, this new, healthier point of view can alter your appearance. A new joy can fill your days, a new quickness can enliven your step, and a new twinkle can sparkle in your eyes.

You are the master of your fate and a more powerful and exciting person than you ever realized. This new power will give you a magnetism that others can't help but respond to. New romantic partners will appear in response to your healthier energy, and they will enjoy basking in the radiant glow of your beautiful, enhanced light.

Yes, the Tarot has answers about your life as it stands now. But it also has the power to help you create a better future through the understanding and application of its marvelously life-affirming teachings.

This is your chance not only to master the universe, but to master yourself. It is a worthwhile pursuit that grants true joy, peace, and a life filled with light and love.

ABOUT THE AUTHOR

NANCY FREDERICK SUSSAN is an astrologer who writes about a variety of metaphysical topics. Her articles appear frequently in every astrology magazine on the stands. She is the editor of *Astro Signs*, read daily by upward of half a million people across the U.S. and Canada. Ms. Sussan recently relocated from New York to beautiful Los Angeles, where she writes, teaches astrology, and counsels a large private clientele.

In your quest for true love, let the heavens help you!
Bantam Books presents

the LOVE LIFE GUIDES

A fun, sexy, and uninhibited series of forecasts, predictions, and compatibility guides for finding and keeping the perfect mate.

Starring Your Love Life: This comprehensive astrology guide includes compatibility match-ups and teasing strategies for attracting that perfect lover—no matter what their sign!

It All Adds Up to Love: Find romance by the numbers! The ancient science of numerology provides scintillating information and understanding of the most important numbers in life and love.

The Lover's Dream: Yes, dreams of love can come true! Learn to interpret and reprogram your dreams to solve your love dilemmas or find the perfect mate.

Tarot: Love is in the Cards: Unveil the mystery of the centuries-old Tarot, and discover how to stack the deck in your favour for love!